The Guide to Basic
RESUME
WRITING

PUBLIC LIBRARY
ASSOCIATION
A division of the American Library Association

The Public Library Association and the Editors of VGM Career Books

The Guide to Basic
RESUME
WRITING

SECOND EDITION

VGM Career Books

Chicago   New York   San Francisco   Lisbon   London   Madrid   Mexico City
Milan   New Delhi   San Juan   Seoul   Singapore   Sydney   Toronto

Library of Congress Cataloging-in-Publication Data

The guide to basic resume writing / PLA and the editors of VGM Career Books.—
3rd ed.
        p.   cm.
Includes bibliographical references.
ISBN 0-07-14059107
    1. Resumes (Employment)—Handbooks, manuals, etc.   I. Title: Basic resume writing.   II. Title: Resume writing.   III. Public Library Association.
IV. VGM Career Books (Firm).

HF5383.G727   2003
650.14'2—dc21   2003049745

2 3 4 5 6 7 8 9 0   QPD/QPD   2 1 0 9 8 7 6 5 4

ISBN 0-07-140591-7

McGraw-Hill books are available at special quantity discounts to use as premiums and sales promotions, or for use in corporate training programs. For more information, please write to the Director of Special Sales, Professional Publishing, McGraw-Hill, Two Penn Plaza, New York, NY 10121-2298. Or contact your local bookstore.

This book is printed on acid-free paper.

Contents

TM

Acknowledgments

The Job and Career Information Services Committee of the Adult Lifelong Learning Section of the Public Library Division of the American Library Association prepared the first edition of the *Guide to Basic Resume Writing*. Contributing members of this committee at the time of the book's initial publication (and their affiliation at that time) included the following:

Marianne Fairfield, Cuyahoga County (Ohio) Public Library; Barbara Fellows, Public Library of Columbus and Franklin County (Ohio); Vera A. Green, Carnegie Library of Pittsburgh; Steven P. Lane, Army Technical Information Center, Fort Lewis, Washington; Jeanne Patterson, Cuyahoga County (Ohio) Public Library; Erlinda Regner, Chicago Public Library; Mary Jo Ryan, Nebraska Library Commission; Ricky Fairtile-Wasserman, Queensborough (New York) Public Library.

Other persons who played important roles in developing the initial version of this book included Marianne Fairfield and Jeanne Patterson, who edited the manuscript; Virginia Fore, Enoch Pratt, and Jane Heiser, State Library of California, who checked the vocabulary; Laura Fliger and Brenda Corder, who contributed resumes; Nancy Fisher, John Lonsak, and Hedy Werner, who worked on final preparation and proofreading; and Nancy Henry, who typed the original manuscript.

We also acknowledge and thank all the public and academic libraries that submitted sample resumes.

The second edition of the *Guide to Basic Resume Writing* was undertaken by the Editors of VGM Career Books in tandem with the Public Library Association. The editors also wish to thank Mark Rowh for his valuable assistance with this second edition.

Foreword

In promoting the expansion of the public library movement in the United States, one of the chief goals behind Andrew Carnegie's widespread philanthropy was the creation of an uniquely American institution that would someday evolve into the "people's university." Through the years, the American public library has clung fast to this goal, offering an array of informational services and lifelong learning opportunities for individuals from infancy through advanced old age that serve to support and enhance a variety of human undertakings.

When initially focusing on the contemporary public library, many may fail to fully realize the tremendous career-related offerings available at almost any public library: occupational guides, business/organizational reports, resume preparation materials, and—perhaps the most essential resource of all—trained and experienced librarians to aid library users in better identifying and utilizing the informational tools needed in their job-seeking pursuits. Now, under the auspices of the Job and Career Information Services Committee of the Public Library Association (a division of the American Library Association), librarians, who are the ultimate information providers, have compiled a resume-writing guide that is our profession's consummate response to its commitment to assist with lifelong learning activities—including career enhancement.

Whether you are considering a job or career change, reentering the job market following a long- or short-term absence, or seeking your first job, this thoughtful, complete, and easy-to-use resume guide is the perfect aid for you. Developed by librarians with years of experience in collecting and providing job assistance information, the *Guide to Basic Resume Writing* is one of the best resources available for those seeking employment in today's demanding and highly competitive job market.

Charles M. Brown
Former President
Public Library Association

A Note from the Editors

In the current job market, it is very important to have all of your facts organized before you start your job search, and creating and maintaining an up-to-date resume is the most important step in this process. Everyone, from a professional in upper management to someone just beginning a first job search, will benefit from keeping track of his or her skills and achievements. This basic guide to resume writing has been designed to fill the gap identified by many librarians and professional job counselors who need simple guidelines for resume writing as well as sample resumes from a variety of fields to share with clients. With help from an instructor, this book can be used by adults enrolled in basic education or workplace literacy classes. Other adults, ranging from college students to those with many years of work experience, may wish to use this guide independently. Regardless of the situation, all will benefit from the most current advice from a range of career counseling experts on formatting, content, style, and submission of both paper and electronic resumes.

We wish you the best of luck finding the job of your dreams!

The Editors of VGM Career Books

General Guidelines for Writing Resumes

Your resume is a piece of paper (or an electronic document) that serves to introduce you to the people who will eventually hire you. To write a thoughtful resume, you must thoroughly assess your personality, your accomplishments, and the skills you have acquired. The act of composing and submitting a resume also requires you to carefully consider the companies or individuals that might hire you. What are they looking for, and how can you meet their needs? This book shows you how to organize your personal information and experience into a concise and well-written resume, so that your qualifications and potential as an employee will be understand easily and quickly by a complete stranger.

Writing the resume is just one step in what can be a daunting job-search process, but it is an important element in the chain of events that will lead you to your new position. While you are probably a talented, bright, and charming person, your resume may not reflect these qualities. A poorly written resume can get you nowhere; a well-written resume can land you an interview and potentially a job. A good resume can even lead the interviewer to ask you questions that will allow you to talk about your strengths and highlight the skills you can bring to a prospective employer. Even a person with very little experience can find a good job if he or she is assisted by a thoughtful and polished resume.

Lengthy, typewritten resumes are a thing of the past. Today, employers do not have the time or the patience for verbose documents; they look for tightly composed, straightforward, action-based resumes. Although a one-page resume is the norm, a two-page resume may be warranted if you have had extensive job experience or have changed careers and truly need the space to properly position yourself. If, after careful editing, you still need more than one page to present yourself, it's acceptable to use a second page. A crowded resume that's hard to read would be the worst of your choices.

WHAT IS A RESUME?

An effective resume is composed of information that employers are most interested in knowing about a prospective job applicant. This vital information will be covered by a few essential elements in a fairly abbreviated form. Because of the limited space allowed a resume writer, you must distill all of your skills, education, and work history into a few brief pages. To that end, it is important that you take stock of all of your qualifications and choose the ones most relevant to your prospective employer.

Start by thinking about all your past jobs, activities, and education, including:

- What you have learned

- Responsibilities you have assumed

- What you have accomplished

- How you have contributed

- Why you have been effective

- All of your abilities and skills

- Where and when you went to school

- Special training

- Certificates and licenses you have earned

Highlighting your skills and accomplishments may seem like bragging, but it is appropriate and even necessary to do so in a resume. Your resume tells the employer about you, and also about the value you place on your skills. Because we are not used to judging ourselves in this way, we sometimes sell ourselves short by downplaying or failing to mention important skills.

WORK HISTORY

Work experience is arguably the most important element of them all. Unless you are a recent graduate or former homemaker with little or no relevant work experience, your current and former positions will provide the central focus of the resume. You will want this section to be as complete and carefully constructed as possible. By thoroughly examining your work experience, you can get to the heart of your accomplishments and present them in a way that demonstrates and highlights your qualifications.

If you are just entering the workforce, your resume will probably focus on your education, but you should also include information on your work or volunteer experiences. Although you will have less information about work experience than a person who has held multiple positions or is advanced in his or her career, the amount of information is not what is most important in this section. How the information is presented and what it says about you as a worker and a person is what really counts.

As you create this section of your resume, remember the need for accuracy. Include all the necessary information about each of your jobs, including your job title, dates of employment, name of your employer, city, state, responsibilities, special projects you handled, and accomplishments. Be sure to list only accomplishments for which you were directly responsible. And don't be alarmed if you haven't participated in or worked on special projects, because this section may not be relevant to certain jobs.

The most common way to list your work experience is in *reverse chronological order*. In other words, start with your most recent job and work your way backward. This way, your prospective employer sees your current (and often most important) position before considering your past employment. Your most recent position, if it's the most important in terms of responsibilities and relevance to the job for which you are applying, should also be the one that includes the most information as compared to your previous positions.

Even if the work itself seems unrelated to your proposed career path, you should list any job or experience that will help "sell" your talents. If you were promoted or given greater responsibilities or commendations, be sure to mention the fact.

EDUCATION AND TRAINING

Education is usually the second most important element of your resume. Your educational background is often a deciding factor in an employer's decision to interview you. Highlight your accomplishments in school as much as you did those accomplishments at work. If you are looking for your first professional job, your education or life experience will be your greatest assets because your related work experience will be minimal. In this case, the education section becomes the most important means of selling yourself.

Include in this section all the degrees or certificates you have received; your major or area of concentration; all of the honors you earned; and any relevant activities you participated in, organized, or chaired. Again, list your most recent schooling first. If you have completed graduate-level work, begin with that and work your way back through your undergraduate education. If you have completed college, you generally should not list your high school experience; do so only if you earned special honors, you had a grade point average that was much better than the norm, or this was your highest level of education.

If you have completed a large number of credit hours in a subject that may be relevant to the position you are seeking but did not obtain a degree, you may wish to list the hours or classes you completed. Keep in mind, however, that you may be asked to explain why you did not finish the program. If you are currently in school, list the degree, certificate, or license you expect to obtain and the projected date of completion.

SPECIAL WORK-RELATED SKILLS AND ACCOMPLISHMENTS

When describing your job duties under each of your previous positions on your resume, you should include specific work-related skills and accomplishments. These might include a fluency in various computer programs, the ability to operate special machinery or equipment, and experience supervising another worker or a work crew. In addition, are there any special accomplishments you've made in your current position? If so, you should be sure to highlight how you've benefited your current employer, which gives prospective employers a glimpse of what you can do for them. For example, helping increase sales or income during any of your jobs; working full time or managing a home while taking courses to complete your diploma or degree; or completing a difficult building project.

ACTIVITIES

Perhaps you have been active in different organizations or clubs; often an employer will look at such involvement as evidence of initiative, dedication, and good social skills. Examples of your ability to take a leading role in a group should be included on a resume, if you can provide them. The activities section of your resume should present neighborhood and community activities, volunteer positions, and so forth. In general, you may want to avoid listing any organization whose name indicates the race, creed, sex, age, marital status, sexual orientation, or nation of origin of its members because this could expose you to discrimination.

As your work experience grows through the years, your school activities and honors will carry less weight and be emphasized less in your resume. Eventually, you will probably list only your degree and any major honors received. As time goes by, your job performance and the experience you've gained become the most important elements in your resume, which should change to reflect this.

CERTIFICATES AND LICENSES

If your chosen career path requires specialized training, you may already have certificates or licenses. You should list these if the job you are seeking requires them and you, of course, have acquired them. If you have applied for a license but have not received it, use the phrase "application pending."

License requirements vary by states. If you have moved or are planning to relocate to another state, check with that state's board or licensing agency for all licensing requirements and always make sure that all of the information you list is completely accurate. Locate copies of your certificates and licenses, and check the exact date and name of the accrediting agency.

PROFESSIONAL MEMBERSHIPS

Another potential element in your resume is a section listing professional memberships. Use this section to describe your involvement in professional associations, unions, and similar organizations. It is to your advantage to list any professional memberships that pertain to the job you are seeking. Many employers see your membership as representative of your desire to stay up-to-date and connected in your field. Include the dates of your involvement and whether you took part in any special activities or held any offices within the organization.

SPECIAL SKILLS

The special skills section of your resume is the place to mention any special abilities you have that relate to the job you are seeking. You can use this element to present certain talents or experiences that are not necessarily a part of your education or work experience. Common examples include fluency in a foreign language, extensive travel abroad, or knowledge of a particular computer application. "Special skills" can encompass a wide range of talents, and this section can be used creatively. However, for each skill you list, you should be able to describe how it would be a direct asset in the type of work you're seeking because employers may ask just that in an interview. If you can't think of a way to do this, it may be extraneous information.

PERSONAL INFORMATION

Some people include personal information on their resumes. This is generally not recommended, but you might wish to include it if you think that something in your personal life, such as a hobby or talent, has some bearing on the position you are seeking. This type of information is often referred to at the beginning of an interview, when it may be used as an "icebreaker." Of course, personal information regarding your age, marital status, race, religion, or sexual orientation should never appear on your resume as *personal information*. It should be given only in the context of memberships and activities, and only when doing so would not expose you to discrimination.

REFERENCES

References are not usually given on the resume itself, but a prospective employer needs to know that you have references who may be contacted if necessary. All you need to include is a single sentence at the end of the resume: "References are available upon request," or even simply, "References available." Have a reference list ready—your interviewer may ask to see it! Contact each person on the list ahead of time to see whether it is all right for you to use him or her as a reference and be sure to inform your references of the positions for which you are applying. Have a candid conversation with them about the types of things you think the prospective employer might be looking for in an employee. This way, the person has a chance to think about what to say *before* the call occurs, and this helps ensure that you will obtain the best reference possible.

WRITING YOUR RESUME

Now that you have gathered the information for each section of your resume, it's time to write it out in a way that will get the attention of the reviewer—hopefully, your future employer! The language you use in your resume will affect its success, so you must be careful and conscientious. To begin, you're going to translate the facts you have gathered into the active, precise language of resume writing. You will be aiming for a resume that keeps the reader's interest and highlights your accomplishments in a concise and effective way.

Resume writing is unlike any other form of writing because you're trying to convey drive and results and the work you do every day in just a few short sentences. In addition, although your seventh-grade composition teacher would not approve, the rules of punctuation and sentence building are often completely ignored. Instead, you should try for a functional, direct writing style that focuses on the use of verbs and other words that imply action on your part. Writing with action words and strong verbs characterizes you to potential employers as an energetic, active person, someone who completes tasks and achieves results for his or her work. Resumes that do not make use of action words can sound passive and stale and won't be effective or get the attention of any employer, no matter how qualified the applicant. To write an active, dynamic resume, you'll need to choose words that display your strengths and demonstrate your initiative. See the sample resumes included later in the book and Appendix B for words you can use to describe your job skills and duties in the most active way.

As previously stated, the work experience section is perhaps the most important section of your resume and you should pay particular attention to its construction. One helpful way to build the work experience section is to make use of your actual job description—the written duties and expectations your employers had for a person in your current or former position. Job descriptions are rarely written in proper resume language, so you will have to rework them, but they do include much of the information necessary to create this section of your resume. If you have access to job descriptions for your former positions, you can use the details to construct an action-oriented paragraph. Often, your human resources department can provide a job description for your current position.

In addition, when writing your resume, if you are applying for more than one job, you may need more than one resume because you will have to highlight different skills for different jobs. For example, you may be equally qualified for two fairly different jobs, and each is seeking a candidate with certain skills. To make yourself the most appealing to each employer you'll need to allot more of your valuable resume space to the specific skills and abilities in demand for that employer and downplay others of less importance. To do this effectively, you'll need to make sure you've thoroughly researched the job description as well as the businesses and companies to which you're applying.

WHAT TO (AND WHAT NOT TO) INCLUDE

- Include a career or job objective if it's specific. If your objective is general, instead include a summary of skills and qualifications.

- Include all work experience and education.

- Include any strengths and accomplishments in your job descriptions.

- Do not list salaries for any job.

- Do not include personal information, such as date of birth, marital status, religion, ethnic group, height, weight, or health.

- Do not include names of supervisors or references. You may end your resume with the statement "References available on request," but this is optional and can be omitted if you have space concerns.

- Do not use the word *Resume* on the top of the page.

ASSEMBLY

At this point, you've gathered all the necessary information for your resume and rewritten it in language that will impress your potential employers. Your next step is to assemble the sections in a logical order and lay them out on the page neatly and attractively to achieve the desired effect: getting the interview.

The order of the elements in a resume makes a difference in its overall effect. Clearly, you would not want to bury your name and address somewhere in the middle of the resume. Nor would you want to lead with a less important section, such as special skills. Put the elements in an order that stresses your most important accomplishments and the things that will be most appealing to your potential employer. For example, if you are new to the workforce, you will want the reviewer to read about your education and life skills before any part-time jobs you may have held for short durations. On the other hand, if you have been gainfully employed for several years and currently hold an important position in your company, you should list your work accomplishments ahead of your educational information, which has become less pertinent with time.

Certain things should always be included in your resume, but others are optional, as previously discussed. Your choice of optional sections depends on your own background and employment needs. Always use information that will put you in a favorable light—unless it's absolutely essential, avoid anything that will prompt the interviewer to ask questions about your weaknesses or something else that could be unflattering. Make sure your information is accurate and truthful. If your honors are impressive, include them in the resume. If your activities in school demonstrate talents that are necessary for the job you are seeking, allow space for a section on activities. If you are applying for a position that requires ornamental illustration, you may want to include border illustrations or graphics that demonstrate your talents in this area. If you are answering an advertisement for a job that requires certain physical traits, a photo of yourself might be appropriate, however, a person applying for a job as a computer programmer would *not* include a photo as part of his or her resume. Each resume is unique, just as each person is unique.

RESUME FORMATS

While there is no single standard resume format, the format you choose can make a difference in the impression you make. It is important to choose a design and approach that is concise and effective and highlights the skills your prospective employer is looking for in an applicant. For example, place education before work experience if you're fresh out of school or use a summary of skills instead of a job objective if you want to highlight your skills over your previous jobs. In order to determine how to best position your skills and accomplishments, ask yourself these questions:

- What in my background best proves I can do the job?

- Should I put my emphasis on my skills, or where I've worked, or on the courses that I've taken in school?

- What are my major selling points?

There are two basic types of resumes, chronological and functional. A chronological resume highlights your work history by date, and a functional resume highlights your skills.

CHRONOLOGICAL FORMAT

A chronological format is useful when the amount of time on each job (paid or unpaid) may be viewed as a strength, your work experience prepares you for your job objective, former job titles or employers are impressive, or you want to show your advancement in a company or a field of work.

The body of a chronological resume includes a listing of your work history, beginning with your most current job. Other sections may include a job objective; information on your education; a summary of skills; volunteer experiences, unions, and other work-related associations; and community activities. Keep in mind that information near the top of the page gets read most carefully. It can be effective to state your job objective and/or your qualifications in a sentence or two before presenting your work history.

The section on work history may be titled *Work History*, *Job History*, *Employment*, or *Experience*. List your latest employment first, then previous jobs according to dates. State your job title, employer, and dates of employment for each job. You may include addresses, but use city and state only. Full addresses will be presented on the reference page.

Under each job title explain exactly what your duties and responsibilities were, what skills you learned, and what you achieved. It is important to use words that tell how much, how often, how well, and what results were produced.

List your formal education and training in a section titled *Education*, *Training*, or *Education and Training*. Typically, the most recent schooling is listed first. This section may be presented either before or after your work history. It will depend on which is most important in the qualifications the employer is looking for.

FUNCTIONAL FORMAT

A functional resume is useful when you want to change career fields and need to identify skills that may be used in a new situation, you have limited work experience but still have skills that can be identified and grouped, you want to enter or reenter paid employment and have acquired skills through unpaid or paid experience, or you have had many different work experiences that are not directly related to the job you're seeking—for example managing a pet shop, repairing appliances, serving as a teacher's aide.

The body of a functional resume highlights your major skill areas. Emphasis is placed on your skills, not on work experience. Job titles, dates, or names of employers may be left out. However, other sections may include a job objective, information on education, a summary of abilities, and memberships and other work-related associations. You may label the section describing your skills in a variety of ways, such as:

- Skills

- Abilities

- Accomplishments

- Experience

- Areas of Competence

Cluster your skills gained through both paid and unpaid experiences under one heading. For example, if you provided word processing on one job, did filing on another job, and acted as a receptionist someplace else, these activities could be listed under the heading of *Office Skills*. In addition, unpaid experience may be listed in the same way. An example of an effective way of presenting this type of information follows.

OFFICE SKILLS

• Using Microsoft Office suite, prepared correspondence and reports for administrative staff of two small companies.

• Established and maintained an effective filing system with over 350 regular customers (auto service center).

• Acted as receptionist in local bank and front office of auto service center.

Use descriptive statements to show your skills—statements that specify (how much? or how often?) and qualify (how well? or results achieved?). Include a section listing your formal education, putting your most recent first.

WHAT A RESUME SHOULD LOOK LIKE

A great deal of care—and much more formatting—is necessary to achieve an attractive layout for your paper resume. And, while there is no single appropriate layout that applies to every resume, there are a few basic rules to follow in putting your resume on paper:

• Leave a comfortable margin on the sides, top, and bottom of the page (usually one to one and a half inches).

• Use appropriate spacing between the sections (two to three line spaces are usually adequate).

• Be consistent in the type of headings you use for different sections of your resume. For example, if you capitalize the heading EMPLOYMENT HISTORY, don't use initial capitals and underlining for a section of equal importance, such as *Education*.

• Do not use more than one font in your resume. Stay consistent by choosing a font that is fairly standard and easy to read, and don't change it for different sections. Beware of the tendency to try to make your resume original by choosing fancy type styles; your resume may end up looking unprofessional instead of creative. Unless you are in a very creative and artistic field, you should almost always stick with tried-and-true type styles like Times New Roman and Palatino, which are often used in business writing. In the area of resume styles, conservative is usually the best way to go.

- Always try to fit your resume on one page. If you are having trouble with this, you may be trying to say too much. Edit out any repetitive or unnecessary information, and shorten descriptions of earlier jobs when possible. Ask a friend you trust for feedback on what seems unnecessary or unimportant. For example, you may have included too many optional sections. Today, with the prevalence of the personal computer as a tool, there is no excuse for a poorly laid out resume. Experiment with variations until you are pleased with the result.

Remember that a resume is not an autobiography. Too much information will only get in the way, and the more compact your resume, the easier it will be to review. If a person who is swamped with resumes looks at yours, catches the main points, and then calls you for an interview to fill in some of the details, your resume has already accomplished its task. A clear and concise resume makes for a happy reader and a good impression.

That said, there are times when, despite extensive editing, the resume simply cannot fit on one page. In this case, the resume should be laid out on two pages in such a way that neither clarity nor appearance is compromised. Each page of a two-page resume should be marked clearly: the first should indicate "Page 1 of 2," and the second should include your name and the page number, for example, "Julia Ramirez—Page 2 of 2." The pages should then be stapled together. You may use a smaller font (in the same font as the body of your resume) for the page numbers. Place them at the bottom of page one and the top of page two. Again, spend the time now to experiment with the layout until you find one that looks good to you.

Always show your final layout to other people and ask them what they like or dislike about it, and what impresses them most when they read your resume. Make sure that their responses are the same as what you want to elicit from your prospective employer. If they aren't the same, you should continue to make changes until the necessary information is emphasized.

Above all, your resume should be eye-catching and easy to read, and it should look professional. If you're concerned about whether or not you can create an effective layout, be aware that many professional resume writing and printing services cost less than you might expect, they are familiar with preparing resumes, and they know how to make a resume look good. That said, laying out your own resume is not as difficult or daunting as you might think. With a little care and consistency anyone can make a professional-looking resume. If you prepare your resume on your own, keep the following tips in mind:

- Highlight the points you want the reader to notice.

- Short phrases are easier to read than long sentences and paragraphs.

- Use dashes (—) or dots (. . .) or asterisks (***), different kinds of type, and underlining to guide the eye, but be sure not to make it too crowded.

- Line up major headings to make the resume easy to scan.

- Have at least three other people proofread your resume to make sure all spelling, grammar, punctuation, and information are correct.

- Choose good quality bond paper for your resume. White, ivory, or gray looks best.

- Make sure photocopies of your resume are of high quality.

HOW TO GET THE PROFESSIONAL LOOK

How your resume looks is sometimes almost as important as what your resume says. Be sure to make your resume look as professional as possible by making it both appealing to the eye and easy to follow. Use the following pointers to help you get the professional look that you want.

A heading presents your name, address, and telephone number. Express your creativity in designing a heading. You may also wish to use this heading for cover letters, thank-you notes, and other correspondence. Be sure your name stands out. Here are some examples of headings:

JOHN JONES
222 Maple Street • Solon, Ohio 44139
216/555-9753 • jjones22@xxx.com

Ellen Rodriguez
826 Elm Street
Cleveland, Ohio 44106
216/555-8308
erod@xxx.com

Ellen Rodriguez

826 Elm Street • Cleveland, OH 44106
(216) 555-8308 • erod@xxx.com

DEWANDA JONES

222 Maple Street
Solon, Ohio 44139
216-555-4353
dewandaj@xxx.com

JOB/CAREER OBJECTIVE

It may be helpful to state a job and/or career objective describing the focus of your job search. This objective statement is a summary, or lead statement, for the rest of your resume focuses on what you can do, states how you can be of help to the employer (it is not a statement of personal goals), identifies for the employer where and how you might fit in the organization, and tells the employer that you have definite goals.

If you include a job objective, it is always the first item on your resume following your heading. The objective statement may be labeled *Objective*, *Job Objective*, *Job Target*, *Career Objective*, *Employment Objective*, or *Professional Objective*.

The statement may be one word, a job title, a phrase, a sentence fragment, or a sentence including the job title or career area. The simplest objective statement may be just the name of the position or job area. If you use a sentence it should contain action verbs and tell the employer what you intend to do, such as sell, supervise, clean, fix, build, or operate.

Avoid general statements, such as "Seeking a responsible position in a progressive organization with opportunity for advancement." Such statements fail to tell the employer anything useful or specific about you or your desires. The following are examples of job/career objective statements:

OBJECTIVE: A position managing a small medical office using my supervisory, organizational, and secretarial skills.

Teo Knauth

1121 frisch · Madison WI 53711

Career Objective

Transportation Coordinator or Supervisor, using management experience and communication skills.

OBJECTIVE

Industrial Sales
Computer Programmer–Systems Analyst

Objective

A position in production using my background in computerized and noncomputerized assembly

QUALIFICATIONS SUMMARY

This brief summary of your qualifications, background, and strengths will highlight information about you that you want an employer to know. Place the qualifications summary immediately following the job/career objective statement or use it in place of one if you're concerned about space. In order to create an effective summary, ask yourself what you most want an employer to know about you, list the ideas you want to get across, and translate your specific experiences into general abilities. These experiences may include length and type of work, personality characteristics, special areas of expertise, and education/training. Here are some examples of qualifications summaries:

SUMMARY

Three years experience with computerized assembly line production, ten years experience as a journeyman machinist

QUALITY CONTROL/MANUFACTURING TECHNICIAN

Qualifications

- 1 year Quality Control Technician
- 8 years Manufacturing Technician
- Worked with statistical quality control, material efficiency, labor efficiency, and random sampling
- Involved in research and development of new products in quartz semiconductor industry

A position in management that will utilize my administrative and supervisory experience

Experience in:

- Administration
- Forecasting
- Recruiting and Training
- Credit Underwriting
- Loan Organization
- Secondary Market Operation

BODY OF THE RESUME

The body of the resume allows you to showcase your experience (paid and unpaid) and your skills. Compiling information for this section was discussed earlier in this chapter, but for now we're focusing on the format of this section. Remember these important guidelines while writing the body of your resume:

- Start with the most important or most time-consuming task.

- Use action verbs to describe tasks.

- Be consistent in use of verb tense, at least in each section. For a current job, use the present tense (develop, organize) or say "Responsible for" (developing, organizing). Use past tense (developed, organized) for former experience.

- Think beyond your everyday responsibilities. List the things you feel good about having done and examples of recognition you have received.

- Choose concise, short, postcard-like phrases.

- Tell quantity information (how much? how many?) showing what you did and how well you did it.

- When describing skills, choose a word or phrase to head each category. Similar activities, experiences, responsibilities, and tasks should be grouped together.

EDUCATION

The section on educational background should include all your formal training, workshops, seminars, and informal training that relate to the job for which you are applying. List apprenticeships and on-the-job training in this section, also.

You may place this section anywhere in the resume, depending on how important you think your education is. For example, if you've recently graduated from a program of study and haven't had any related work experience, you may place your educational achievements near the top of the resume. If you haven't been in school for a few years, you may want to place your education section after your work experience section, at the end of the resume.

No matter where you place the section on education, be sure to include:

- Educational and training experiences (most recent first)

- Workshops, seminars, and continuing education programs that relate to your objective

- Apprenticeships and on-the-job training

- School-related activities, such as honors, offices held, and significant activities, if they are related to your objective

- The name of the institution, its location, your diploma or certification or degree, and dates of completion

If you attended college, mention college courses taken, college major and minor, and any special requirements met, if they are related to your objective. Also, consider mentioning any college or training expenses you earned on your own.

ELECTRONIC RESUMES

If you are planning to use this resume online, or you suspect your potential employer is likely to scan your resume, you will want to include a *keyword* in the objective. This allows a prospective employer, searching hundreds of resumes for a specific skill or position objective, to locate the keyword and find your resume. In essence, a keyword is what's "hot" in your particular field at a given time. It's a buzzword, a shorthand way of getting a particular message across at a glance. For example, if you are a lawyer, you might mention in your objective your desire to work in the area of corporate litigation. In this case, someone searching for the keyword *corporate litigation* will pull up your resume and know that you want to plan, research, and present cases at trial on behalf of the corporation. If your objective states that you "desire a challenging position in systems design," the keyword is *systems design*, an industry-specific, shorthand way of saying that you want to be involved in assessing the need for, acquiring, and implementing high-technology systems. Every industry has keywords, and it's becoming more and more important to include a few in your resume. You may need to conduct additional research to make sure you know what keywords are most likely to be used in your desired industry, profession, or situation.

There are many resume and job-search sites online. Like most things in the online world, they vary a great deal in quality. Use your discretion. If you plan to apply for jobs online or advertise your availability this way, you will want to design a scannable resume. This type of resume uses a format that can be easily scanned into a computer and added to a database. Scanning allows a prospective employer to use keywords to quickly review each applicant's experience and skills, and (in the event that there are many candidates for the job) to keep your resume for future reference.

Many people find that it is worthwhile to create two or more versions of their basic resume. You may want an intricately designed resume on high-quality paper to mail or hand out and a resume that is designed to be scanned into a computer and saved on a database or an online job site. You can even create a resume in ASCII text to E-mail to prospective employers. For further information, you may wish to refer to the *Guide to Internet Job Searching*, by Frances Roehm and Margaret Dikel, updated and published every other year by VGM Career Books, a division of the McGraw-Hill Companies. This excellent book contains helpful and detailed information about formatting a resume for Internet use. To get you started, following is a list of things to keep in mind when creating electronic resumes.

SPECIAL TIPS FOR ELECTRONIC RESUMES

Because there are many details to consider in writing a resume that will be posted or transmitted on the Internet, or one that will be scanned into a computer when it is received, we suggest that you refer to the *Guide to Internet Job Searching*, by Frances Roehm and Margaret Dikel, as previously mentioned. However, here are some brief general guidelines to follow if you expect your resume to be scanned into a computer.

- Use standard fonts in which none of the letters touch.

- Keep in mind that underlining, italics, and fancy scripts may not scan well.

- Use boldface and capitalization to set off elements. Again, make sure letters don't touch. Leave at least a quarter inch between lines of type.

- Keep information and elements at the left margin. Centering, columns, and even indenting may change when the resume is optically scanned.

- Do not use any lines, boxes, or graphics.

- Place the most important information at the top of the first page. If you use two pages, put "Page 1 of 2" at the bottom of the first page and put your name and "Page 2 of 2" at the top of the second page.

- List each telephone number on its own line in the header.

- Use multiple keywords or synonyms for what you do to make sure your qualifications will be picked up if a prospective employer is searching for them. Use nouns rather than verbs that are keywords for your profession.

- Be descriptive in your titles. For example, don't just use "assistant"; use "legal office assistant."

- Make sure the contrast between print and paper is good. Use a high-quality laser printer and white or very light colored 8½-by-11-inch paper.

- Mail a high-quality laser print or an excellent copy. Do not fold or use staples, as this might interfere with scanning. You may, however, use paper clips.

In addition to creating a resume that works well for scanning, you may want to have a resume that can be E-mailed to reviewers. Because you may not know what word processing application the recipient uses, the best format to use is ASCII text. ASCII stands for "American Standard Code for Information Exchange." It allows people with very different software platforms to exchange and understand information. (E-mail operates on this principle.) ASCII is a simple, text-only language, which means you can include only simple text. There can be no use of boldface, italics, or even paragraph indentations.

To create an ASCII resume, just use your normal word processing program; when finished, save it as a "text only" document. You will find this option under the "save" or "save as" command. Here is a list of things to *avoid* when crafting your electronic resume:

- Tabs. Use your space bar. Tabs will not work.

- Any special characters, such as mathematical symbols.

- Word wrap. Use hard returns (the return key) to make line breaks.

- Centering or other formatting. Align everything at the left margin.

- Bold or italics fonts. Everything will be converted to plain text when you save the file as a "text only" document.

Check carefully for any mistakes before you save the document as a text file. Check spelling and proofread it several times; then ask someone with a keen eye to go over it again for you. Remember: the key is to keep it simple. Any attempt to make this resume pretty or decorative may result in a resume that is confusing and hard to read. After you have saved the document, you can cut and paste it into an E-mail or onto a website.

Part II

Advice from the Experts

Although anyone can learn to develop an effective resume, it can also be helpful to consult those who specialize in the career search process. In this spirit, the following are common resume and cover letter questions posed to career counselors and other experts, and their responses. Some have chosen to answer only one or two questions, while others have weighed in on a number of topics, providing a variety of helpful tips and advice.

In considering the advice provided, keep in mind that there is room for different approaches to resume development depending on your work and education experiences as well as the career path you are pursuing. In fact, even the experts sometimes disagree about the finer points of writing effective resumes. This is an indicator that some flexibility in constructing a resume is possible and should set you at ease in building your own outstanding resume.

Good luck in your job search!

How long should my resume be?

Michele Lobianco, Resume Deli, New York, NY: Employers rapidly sort through resumes in thirty seconds or less before selecting those that are worthy of a second look. As a result, a resume must communicate a candidate's most relevant qualifications in a succinct, easy-to-read format. This can typically be done in one to two pages.

Although there are no hard-and-fast rules, generally a job seeker with less than eight years of experience should stick to a one-page resume, whereas an individual with more than eight years of experience can add a second page. It is rarely necessary for a resume to be longer than two pages since most employers are only interested in the last ten to fifteen years of the candidate's achievements.

In a few fields, most notably academia, a resume—also referred to as a *CV* or *curriculum vitae*—can be much longer. This type of resume is typically a more exhaustive list of experience, presentations, publications, fellowships, and so forth.

Christine Earman Harriger, Career Counselor, George Mason University, Fairfax, VA: A good rule of thumb is that a resume should be as long as it needs to be to adequately match yourself to the position for which you are applying. The rule of keeping a resume to only one page could be broken if your experience and education merits more length.

For example, if you are trying to show how some former work experience prepares you for a position, then you need to determine an appropriate format that will allow you to include it on your resume. So, lay out the work history section of your resume accordingly to allow for certain experiences to be included.

Please note, everyone has a difference work history. The resume of somebody who has worked in one position for twenty years will look drastically different from an entry-level job seeker who has had six jobs in eight years. Try experimenting with different types of resumes, such as a functional or hybrid resume, to highlight your experience.

Last, remember that the resume gets you the interview . . . the interview gets you the job!

Your resume needs to include enough information to pique the curiosity of the interviewer and help you qualify for the position, but not so much information that it is time-consuming and difficult to read.

Dr. Joan Baum, Director, Professional Development, Marymount Manhattan College, New York, NY: For most entry-level jobs, meaning right after college, one page. For sophisticated positions, usually requiring years of experience and graduate or professional degrees, the resume can and should be longer. If you are in a performance field, such as acting, dance, painting, and so on, you should have a performance resume, but it should not be sent. It should, however, be noted, as in "performance resume available on request." When you are asked in for an interview, bring along not only the traditional resume but the performance resume as well. Remember: the resume is merely an eye-catcher. The clincher is the interview or round of interviews (and you should bring along extra copies of the resume in case you are interviewed by more than one person).

Lena Bottos, Compensation Consultant, Salary.com, Wellesley, MA: One page. Your resume is a summary of the highlights of your career and education; it's not a detailed autobiography. The more you include the less likely it is that the potential employer will find those one or two critical experiences that make you the strongest candidate for the position. When you extend your resume beyond one page, you run the risk that anything on the subsequent pages may never be seen.

You break no laws going onto a second page, but if you are going to do it make it worthwhile. Certainly don't tack on a second page for just one sentence or bullet point; move your margins to make it fit. And never print a two-page resume double-sided—you will run an enormous risk that the second page will never be seen.

A two-page resume is acceptable if you have a long career, special accomplishments, or a laundry list of certifications that need to be communicated. Just remember your resume is not an autobiography. The goal is communicate enough information about your accomplishments to tease the reader into extending an invitation for an interview.

Note: It is expected and accepted for academic and technical research people to use a multiple-page resume, which is commonly called a *curriculum vitae.*

Tanya K. Bodzin, Career and Life Coach, Alexandria, VA: This is a loaded question. Most people have heard of the one page rule. When I see resumes that are on one page written in 9 point font and less than one-half inch border, I know immediately that the writer is trying desperately to keep to the one page rule. I have never seen a resume on one page that does the writer justice. These one-pagers are so difficult to read that an employer will trash it immediately because he or she can't read the darn thing. And the writer has slaved over this resume all for naught. Appearance of the resume is important. Why? It is an advertisement of the job seeker and what he or she can do for the prospective employer. What does that mean? Like most advertisements it should be sharp, clean, pleasing to the eye, readable, and have lots of white space. A prospective reader should want to pick up the resume because it looks attractive, has bullets, clear descriptions of accomplishments, and lots of applicable buzzwords.

Most screeners of resumes have difficulty reading a small font—reason number one for using a 12 point font. Even if sent electronically, most companies require a 10 to 12 point font for submission. White space, large enough font, buzzwords, content, and organization all come into play. To do oneself justice with great samples of accomplishments the job seeker needs a resume that is more than one page. One page can only offer a *profile* of the job seeker, and that is another marketing instrument altogether.

What should I do if I have limited work experience?

Joyce Picard, Director, Career Counseling Associates, Newton, MA: Depending on where you are coming from this may not be as great an issue as it appears on the surface. For example, if you are a recent college graduate you may not be expected to have a rich chronological resume since you would be a candidate for an entry professional position, perhaps in administration, marketing, development, or at the specialist level in software development, and so on. Academic record, skill sets, lower status needs, and good communication skills may be the more relevant. On the other hand, should you be five to ten years out of college and having done a "my thing experience," then limited work experience would be a major issue for most salaried/professional level positions.

In any case the way of handling the limited experience issue on the resume is to present yourself in the "what I can do for you" format. In the *Objective* section of the document citing a specific target occupation and role is most desirable. Next, a heading of *Qualifications* may work.

- Proven performance in relating to all levels of work force up to professional level.
- Strong technical skills including Word, Excel, etc.
- Verbal and business writing skills including correspondence, reports, and presentations.
- Quantitative skills including bookkeeping, ratios, and statistics.
- Personal qualities: self-starter, multitask, dependable and affable team player.

For a recent college graduate the school and sampling of courses relevant to the position would follow next. With limited experience the next section should be titled *Experience* and not *Work History*. This section may be chronological or grouped by categories. Under each experience, bullet accomplishments.

The other option would be to go with a straight functional resume. You may highlight in bullet fashion under your personal identification how you would like to be perceived by the reader.

- visual artist
- graphics
- multiple software
- merchandising

This may be followed by several (three at most) categories with accomplishments in bullet form such as:

Merchandising

*

*

Promotion

*

*

Technical

*

*

This to be followed by the work history. Attention in this resume is drawn to skills.

Susan W. Miller, Master Career Counselor, California Career Services, Los Angeles, CA: If you are a recent college graduate or have completed or are currently enrolled in job-specific training, list your relevant course work, any honors or awards you have received, and internships and student memberships in professional associations or other related affiliations. In addition, you can list any relevant research you have conducted or papers you have written, your leadership and community or volunteer experience, and other special qualifications such as foreign language fluency and any computer software programs that you know.

Liz Ryan, CEO and Founder, WorldWIT, Boulder, CO: It's OK to have limited work experience. Employers are always looking for people with less experience because, very honestly, they cost less, and because employers are less worried about losing these people to a better job whenever the economy makes a slight improvement.

Karen S. McAndrew, Director, Office of Career Services, Harvey Mudd College, Claremont, CA: If you have limited work experience, you can be creative in describing the work experience you do have. Employers value "soft" skills such as good communication (oral and written), initiative, enthusiasm, flexibility, dependability, and so on, and these abilities may be demonstrated in the way you describe your experience. Additionally, "work experience" does not translate to "paid work." Volunteer work or projects/hobbies that demonstrate skills relevant to the position for which you are applying can be listed and described on your resume.

Michael F. Courteau, Career Development Instructor, The Art Institutes International Minnesota, Minneapolis, MN: If you have limited work experience to list on your resume, create a functional resume that emphasizes skills. Thus, near the top of your resume, create a section entitled *Skills*, and list such items as particular software knowledge (for example, Adobe Photoshop and Illustrator), bilingual skills (Spanish, Russian), and mechanical skills (TIG welding, punch press). In addition, you can also use a functional resume to emphasize your educational background. Focusing on skills and education is an effective way to address the issue of limited work experience.

Evan Burks, Senior Vice President, Comforce Corporation, Woodbury, NY: Focus on areas that demonstrate your positive traits. For instance, educational accomplishments should be highlighted. In fact, you may even want to list these before work experience. A customized objective (to the job) is also appropriate. It not only sends the message that you want the job, but also gives you an opportunity to showcase your writing skills.

Tracy Gartmann, Director of the Center for Calling and Career and Director of Placement, Maryville College, Maryville, TN: Recent college graduates (and others as well) who have limited employment experience should make the most of their educational experiences by using an effective format that highlights their time in school. For example, the following standardized format ensures that the student is communicating a significant level of commitment to his or her education by listing earned and awarded scholarships, honors, awards, and dedication to helping afford the degree.

B.A., May 2003, Maryville College, Maryville, Tennessee
Major: Business and Organization Management
Minor: Sociology
Honors: Dean's List, 5 semesters
Church & College Scholar
All-Academic Varsity Basketball Team
Most Outstanding Ecology Student, 2001
Omicron Delta Kappa, National Leadership Honor Society
Grade Point Average: 3.6/4.0 [Or: Major GPA: 3.6/4.0]
24% of Total College Expenses Earned While Enrolled

Your overall grade point average should be listed if it is above a 3.0/4.0. If lower, it is better to use your grade point average in your major, assuming it will be much higher.

When should college students begin developing a resume?

Evan Burks: Junior or senior year. You'll gain experience, as well as more time to have others critique your resume. Starting the process—just sitting down and actually doing it—can be the most difficult part. But think of the head start you'll have on others who waited until after they graduated.

What should I do if I have a gap in employment?

Dr. Peter A. Manzi, National Certified Career Counselor and Master Career Counselor, Rochester, NY: The length of the gap and the activities that preceded it and followed it are important contextual factors. If the gap was a brief and atypical blip on the screen, no harm is apparent. Longer gaps are more noticeable than shorter gaps, and a series of gaps, however brief each is, is even more problematic. In some cases, using a functional resume may be one approach to minimize long or multiple gaps in employment. This entails not listing any dates for work-related activities, but describing them as a series of work functions, such as sales, management, customer relations, and so on.

There are some who feel a functional resume is a red flag, but a lot depends on what the person did during the gap and the other sets of skills and experiences he or she developed outside the gap. If a person was incarcerated or in a drug rehabilitation program, that does raise a potential problem and these issues will have to be addressed carefully. Some employers are more tolerant and understanding of applicants going through rough or difficult times than others. If a person had a disability or illness of any type that precluded her or him from gainful work, that too is an important issue that will need to be thoughtfully weighed. If a person chose to raise a family, care for an ill family member, or cites other helping reasons, there is far less negativity associated with these reasons behind a gap.

A lot will also depend on the type of position for which one applies. A gap in employment is less damaging if the sought position is an entry-level one, or one in a new field. For example, if one worked as a salesperson for three years, followed by a nonemployment gap of two years, and then applied for an entry-level position as a customer service representative in a supermarket chain, the gap would not be scrutinized as much as if the person applied for another sales position. Some employers favor continued experience in the same field, while others may want a person with a fresh or different background. In this example, the gap could be minimized if the person engaged in any kind of customer contact or public interaction activities, even if they were not remunerated. For example, many organizations have board members and committee designees who use and develop customer service skills such as problem solving, conflict resolution, staff communication, and so forth. A gap based on unemployment never looks great, but given the state of the economy, it should not seem unreasonable, especially in industries that have been hard hit by economic downturns.

The issue of the gap may or may not be raised in an interview, but the applicant should be well prepared to address it in an open, constructive, and nondefensive way. I had one person who candidly said, "I got out of the rat race in sales because of the stress it was placing on my marriage and family. I decided to work as a sales manager in a local store for a year, because it was close to home and did not involve travel. I then got downsized when the chain declared bankruptcy." When unemployed, it is helpful to engage in positive and healthy activities and achievements, such as joining a health club, continuing education, attending seminars, and so forth. Being a couch potato is perhaps the worst-case scenario when having gaps in employment. Ultimately, employers are more interested in what employees can do for them now, not in what happened in past employment.

A confident, comprehensive assessment of one's skills and assets can overcome many gaps, especially when presented in a way that appears to benefit the company or organization doing the hiring.

Dr. Janet Scarborough, Career Counselor, Bridgeway Career Development, Seattle, WA: Lots of interesting and successful people have gaps in employment. The challenge is to use those gaps to increase rather than threaten one's marketability in a competitive job search. Often those job seekers who have colorful life experiences are the ones who stand out when a hiring manager receives hundreds of resumes for one job opening. I encourage clients who are between jobs to complete education, master athletic or adventure-oriented challenges, or contribute to society through altruistic endeavors. Besides being fun, these experiences can be great for networking and for providing material for interview conversations. On a resume, a job seeker should portray these accomplishments in a straightforward and unapologetic way that communicates pride in achievement, because the employers who will appreciate a diverse background are the exact same high quality employers for whom most people would prefer to work.

Evan Burks: Gaps in excess of a couple of months serve as red flags to most resume reviewers. Even short-term gaps cause questions if they occur frequently. One way to minimize this is to list employment dates in terms of year instead of month and year. This will probably come up during an actual interview, and can be explained at that time.

Where should I go to get help with developing my resume?

David M. Westhart, Director, Career Development Center, Jefferson College of Health Professions, Thomas Jefferson University, Philadelphia, PA: Back to school! Whether it is the career center at the college where you received your degree, or your high school guidance counselor, schools almost always have someone who will help you with your resume.

Most cities also have fee-free help from nonprofit organizations. Here in Philadelphia we have the Philadelphia Workforce Development Corporation, which offers resume and job search help on a walk-in basis. Check the government blue pages in your phonebook for similar organizations.

Dr. Joan Baum: If you are a registered student your college or university will have a career office and your library tons of material. More and more, you can also find wonderful advice and sample materials online, much of it posted by colleges.

If you are not a student, the online material is still there. Then there are always the classics such as the *Parachute* series. Do not throw your money away seeking so-called professional writers. They don't care about you, they won't tailor-make your resume because they will not have time to get to know you, and if they do it for you they will not be helping you to do something you should be doing yourself. This is your life! Take charge.

Liz Ryan: Use your friends and colleagues first, especially if they are in Human Resources positions or hiring roles in their companies. They will give a fresh eye to the information that you are so familiar with, help you clarify terms that might be confusing, and convince you to drop a long-winded description of some great project that you've spent too many words on. Next, review your resume (before it's printed or posted anywhere electronically) with a search professional in your field. Take his or her advice to heart—these are the people who make the yes/no decisions on resumes like yours.

Joseph Terach, Resume Deli, New York, NY: Start close to home. Friends and family can often serve as a second pair of eyes as you develop your resume. A respected colleague is another good resource, so long as you can trust him or her not to tell the boss you're looking for a new job! These are people who have firsthand, intimate knowledge of your work experience, and who are likely familiar with the tasks that give you the greatest satisfaction. Not to mention, this help is free.

That said, if you are serious about your job search, and are willing to invest in your future, professional resume help is easy to access and affordable. Check online, for starters. Resume Deli (resumedeli.com),

Resume.com (resumedeli.com), and Resume Edge (resumeedge.com) are three firms offering online resume services. Resume Deli is unique in that it is primarily staffed by career counselors who are also professional writers and hands-on specialists in most major industries.

You should also investigate your alma mater's career center, which may (or may not) offer resume help to its alumni. But beware of a few potential drawbacks. Though staffed by professional career counselors, many university career centers are grossly understaffed and therefore can only offer minimal assistance. And you may also be forced to pony up steep alumni dues before gaining access to the help you need. In addition, many schools only serve alumni in person so if you live far away you might be out of luck.

Evan Burks: A professional staffing company is familiar with resumes from practically every profession. That is what they do—put people to work. And their stock-in-trade is reading and critiquing resumes.

Should I have a friend or colleague review my resume?

Evan Burks: It always helps to have another pair of eyes—to catch typos, to see if the formatting works, to see if it's easy to read. In addition, colleagues and friends might have a different perspective on your work experience. And they may be able to point out things that you may have overlooked.

Should my resume always have an objective?

Kathy Woughter, Director, Career Development Center, Alfred University, Alfred, NY: Not necessarily. In fact, many experienced professionals find it more advantageous to use a summary of skills instead. This states not what you want from the company, but what you have to offer. Also, if you are including a cover letter, or responding to a posted opening, it should be obvious what your objective is. Last, if you have graduated with a specific degree that implies a certain objective (for example, elementary education, accounting), and you are applying for an entry-level job in that field, you will not need to state it again as a line on your resume.

However, if you're applying to an organization that has multiple openings—or you are prospecting with a company that doesn't have any posted openings—then an objective is probably appropriate.

Dr. Joan Baum: Oftentimes, objectives are either unnecessary because they are so general or inadvisable because too particular, though more often than not it's the first category that is the case. Who wouldn't want a "challenging job that will utilize my skills and training"? Would someone actually want a position where he or she couldn't "grow"? Considering the fact that most resumes take about three seconds to read, why waste time with the obvious? The resume itself should be so specific and concrete that your objective is easily inferred. If the objective is too restricted, however ("Seeking a managerial position in an upscale retail shoe store located in New York City"), the limit does not allow for flexible placement or interdisciplinary development. Most positions these days are not exactly correspondent to college courses and draw on different areas or disciplines. Moreover, technology is changing the look of the workplace and the nature of work. Objectives cannot adequately address these changes.

Liz Ryan: It depends on your field. If you are clearly a salesperson in the software industry, for example, it's not necessary to also say that you want a job as a software salesperson. If your experience is more varied or if you are an inexperienced job seeker, you should include a well-written objective.

Martin Jaffe, Manager, InfoPLACE, Cuyahoga County Public Library, Cleveland, OH: Clients often say to us, "A resume objective limits me and as a multitalented individual I object to reducing my expertise to one catchy sentence." InfoPLACE believes that an objective is an effective method of focusing your expertise on the employer's perspective. The prospective employer is looking for an employee with specific focus in an area of expertise relevant to what the employer will need done. We advocate writing the objective in one of two core methods: either by specific job title with matching relevant skills or by overall focus area with three matching skills. Two examples: first by job title—"Position as a Career Counselor utilizing my individual counseling, assessment/testing, and workshop design expertise." Or by overall career field, "Career/Educational Planning position utilizing my individual counseling, assessment/testing, and workshop design expertise." One of these two core strategies will be effective for anyone writing a resume objective.

Bill Coleman, SVP of Compensation, Salary.com, Wellesley, MA: It is not necessary to have an objective on your summary if your career path is clear from the rest of your resume. Graduating students and other new entrants into the job market whose resumes don't demonstrate a clear career path should consider having an objective to allow the recipient to know what type of position you're looking for. Yes, that may be in your cover letter or it may be clear from the job you're applying for, but it's good to reinforce that message and it's also important to state it in case your resume gets separated from the cover letter or the job posting. You want your resume to be able to stand alone to represent you whether it's in that company's files or if the recipient forwards it to a colleague at another employer.

Tanya K. Bodzin: Your resume should have an objective only if the organization requests one, and then keep it short and direct. A resume is an ad to get you into the interview. Every line of resume is precious to the job seeker in terms of showcasing skills and knowledge that the prospective employer is seeking.

When I review a resume I should be able to tell what kind of job the writer is seeking by the time I have read the first five lines of the resume. I recommend using a skill summary to take the place of a job objective. This is a much better use of space.

Again, the only caveat is does the organization look for job objectives on its applications? If so, then craft one that showcases what you bring to the table, not what you want in your job. The employer doesn't care what you want, the employer wants someone who is technically competent, has experience, and can hit the ground running.

Should my resume always have a summary?

Bill Coleman: A summary can be a good way to highlight the key strengths in your resume. This is especially useful for someone whose resume shows a variety of work experiences. By calling attention to the most important traits that are embedded among one's experiences, a well-worded summary tells the employer what conclusions to draw from reading the rest of the resume. The summary is the employer's take-away.

Should I list references on my resume, or just note that they're available on request?

Kathy Woughter: Neither. It's always implied that references are available upon request, so unless it's specifically requested, don't take up space with reference names, or an unnecessary statement, on your resume. It's OK on some occasions to include a separate reference page, though.

Susan W. Miller: You should list names of references with position title, company address and phone number, and E-mail on a separate page. In addition, it is helpful to have kudos in writing from your references. The letter or E-mail from your references should be written directly to you, not "to whom it may concern" so it looks like a thank-you to you for a job well done and emphasizes your skills and accomplishments. When looking for work, the more marketing materials you have to use for follow-ups, the better!

James K. Elkins, NCCC, MCC, Career Counselor, Career Planning Services, Scarborough, ME: Never list references on a resume, but have a printed list available, including job titles and contact information. If possible, references should not be given out prior to an interview so that you will have the chance to prepare them for questions that a prospective employer might ask. Always contact references before using them and follow up when you feel they may be contacted to provide specific information concerning a position and your relevant skills. Additionally, providing references with a copy of your resume may help them to promote you better.

Jeffrey Taylor, Resume Deli, New York, NY: The names and contact information for your references should be listed on a separate page, not on the resume itself. Recent graduates must generally list at least one professor or teaching assistant, and everyone should list at least one current or past supervisor. Three to five references are sufficient. You might consider listing your references in the order you want them to be called.

Christine Earman Harriger: References do not belong on resumes. Prepare a "reference sheet" on a separate sheet of paper to submit with your resume. Think of your paperwork as your "marketing packet"—include a cover letter, resume, and reference sheet in the packet. Match the heading of the reference sheet to that of your resume and cover letter. All of the documents should look professional and be free of errors.

The reference sheet should include your name and address heading, as well as three to five blocks of contact information for your references. The contact information necessary for your references should include the individual's name, official title, address information, and phone numbers. You may want to include an additional line of text with an asterisk and identify how you know the reference, for example former supervisor, college professor, and so on. You should be prepared to submit the information for three to five references.

Outstanding references are very important. You need to select individuals who support you and your career goals. The best reference is somebody who works in and has excelled in the same type of career path that you are interested in pursuing. It is critical to select a person who knows your background, skills, and value. References can be the final determining factor between you and somebody else getting the job offer.

What items should never be listed on a resume?

Evan Burks: Personal information relating to physical characteristics, marital status, age, sex, or religious affiliation has no place on a resume. Anything that does not relate to your talent and experience only takes up valuable space—and possibly lessens your chances of getting in front of the interviewer.

How important is the selection of font size and style for use in a resume?

Evan Burks: Your resume is first and foremost a personal marketing piece. And here, perception is very definitely reality. The feel and look of your resume is vital. For example, using a cursive font style or italics is just not appropriate; it's not professional, and it's not easy to read. Times Roman or Arial are among commonly accepted typefaces. A lot of this is just plain common sense. If your type size is too large, you'll limit what you can fit on a page; too small, and the page becomes cluttered and hard to read.

Should I include hobbies or other personal information on my resume?

Susan W. Miller: Do not include your age, marital status, or health. This personal data can only be addressed in a job interview if they are BFOQs or bona fide occupational qualifications. Only include hobbies that you are still involved with and enjoy talking about or where you have gained proficiency and/or have received some recognition.

Dr. Joan Baum: No, you shouldn't include personal information on your resume. In case particular activities do seem relevant to the skills or functions of the job, you should provide this information in the cover letter. Resumes should be succinct and fact filled, with information that conveys your education and work. But suppose the job you are applying for is a camp director? Then what might otherwise seem like a hobby—swimming, painting, running—may in this case be part of your experience and will be on your resume as such.

Liz Ryan: You can include one line of *Interests* if you have a fairly blank resume. This is most appropriate for younger people with less job experience. Most employers don't really care or will cover this territory only if you get to the in-person interview stage.

Evan Burks: The only personal information that should be included might relate to special community activities, such as being on the board of directors of a nonprofit organization. Additionally, list awards that might demonstrate teamwork or leadership capabilities.

What's the best format for listing your employers and job titles?

Laura Hill, Managing Director, Client Services, Crenshaw Associates, New York, NY: There is an unwritten standard on this that, when followed, makes your resume easier to read. The company name should always be listed first and at the left margin; ALL CAPS can be a nice way to display it. Provide the location directly after the company name, although you should not use all caps or other emphasis on the location (you want to draw the reader's eyes to company and job title). Put your job title directly below the company name.

COMPANY NAME, City, ST

Job Title

How do I list several different jobs with one company?

Laura Hill: You want to show the reader that you didn't job hop—that you gained varied experiences and (presumably) were promoted along the way. To do this you list the company name once and put the all-inclusive dates at the right margin on the same line as the company name. Then, for specific job assignments you list them under the company heading as follows:

COMPANY NAME, Fargo, SD   1996–2002

Controller, Plastics Division   (2000–2002)

Describe your job and bullet your accomplishments relevant to this assignment.
- Accomplishment
- Accomplishment
- Accomplishment

Fixed Asset Accounting Manager, Power Division   (1998–2002)

Describe your job and bullet your accomplishments relevant to this assignment.
- Accomplishment
- Accomplishment
- Accomplishment

Is using reverse chronological order the best way to organize a resume?

Michele Lobianco: There are two main methods of organizing a resume. These are referred to as the *reverse chronological* (or *chronological* for short) format and the *functional* format. The chronological format—which emphasizes career progression over time—is by far the most frequently used as it is the easiest for most readers to follow. In this format, a candidate's work experience is listed in reverse chronological order, in other words with the most recent position first. Recent studies show that employers and executive recruiters continue to prefer this format to the functional style, because there is no guesswork required when it comes to identifying a person's work history and career progression.

The functional format stresses the job seeker's most marketable skills, but de-emphasizes career progression, job titles, and chronology. This approach works best for career changers with little or no direct experience in the field they are targeting or for individuals who have multiple gaps in their work history. For those pursuing a career change, however, it is critical that they effectively network to gain access to key contacts in their new target field and not simply rely on their resume. Ultimately, the decision regarding whether to use a functional format should always be weighed against the fact that most traditional employers and executive recruiters still prefer the chronological approach to resumes.

Dr. Joan Baum: The only rule should be to do what seems best suited to the job. If you are an older person seeking employment and feel that you are up against age discrimination, then you should arrange your work experience in reverse chronological order but not necessarily put in dates. Reading a chronologically ordered resume is faster—and thus easier—to do, so for this reason alone it is recommended.

Should I pay to have my resume professionally printed?

Dr. Joan Baum: Absolutely not. There is no reason why good old medium-weight bond printing off a Hewlett Packard can't do the job. If you don't have access to a printer, get your resume on a disc and hand it to a friend to print out for you (then take the friend for coffee). If you're typical, you'll be sending out resumes and cover letters all your working life, so you should invest in a printer that is compatible with your computer. The good news is that printers are inexpensive. The better news is that as technological refinements continue, both printers and computers will be even cheaper. People who have their resumes professionally printed usually wind up caring more for the look of the sheet than for the content, and worry over minor considerations such as color. Professional printers may feel they have to earn their keep and do fancy stuff with pictures and letter designs—not a good idea. You never know who will see your resume, and the guideline should be that if you err, let it be on the conservative side.

Liz Ryan: Yes, you should have your resume printed, but that can mean Kinko's or another copy shop, if the paper is a good quality. You do not need to go to an expensive business printer for your resume. A simple font (text style) on white, beige, or pale-blue or pale-gray paper is best. In addition to the hard copy (paper version) of your resume, you should have two other formats. One is a plain-text E-mail version that you'll use when you send your resume to prospective employers. This is important! The third format is to have your resume online. There are a number of sites that will allow you to "park" your resume online. That way, you can let prospective employers know where to find your resume on the Internet. It's much easier than having managers in a company have to shuffle around the E-mail version or, worse yet, the paper version of your resume.

Bill Coleman: Professional printing is not necessary or practical for most people. People interviewing in the printing, graphics, or arts areas may rightly consider professional printing, but most of us are perfectly well served to use a high-quality laser-printed resume (on good quality paper).

A professionally printed resume also has the problem of being a frozen document, whereas a laser-printed resume can be tailored to meet any specific job requirements or stylistic preferences of a specific job.

Regardless of how your resume is printed, remember to photocopy and fax it to yourself to see how well it reproduces because, in all likelihood, most people will see a copy rather than the beautiful original you printed.

How often should I update my resume?

Ellie Augur, Career Counselor, ReadyMinds, New York, NY: Usually, some editing is necessary each time you apply for a job. When at a particular job for a while, it is appropriate to update one's resume. Responsibilities have perhaps changed and you will want to record this so that you always have an updated resume available.

Resumes get attention when they match the job for which one is applying. The following steps will assist in updating a resume:

- Research the company and seek out people who work there or have experience with the company. Talk with them to get a feel for the culture, work, and product.

- Research the position that is open.

- Highlight how your accomplishments and skills match with the requirements for the position.

- While going through this process, be conscious of the benefits you bring to the company and attempt to weave this into your print material.

Dr. Joan Baum: Every time there is a change in your education or your working experience, you should update your resume. You should also have a few versions of your resume where, depending on what kind of job it is that you apply for, you can switch categories around easily. For some jobs, leading with education may make more sense than starting with your work experience. Some positions calling for retail background may cause you to accent your sales work; others, requesting lots of computer savvy, may suggest stressing your data input work. Make sure you destroy earlier resumes so that in a hurry you don't inadvertently send the wrong file—it's been known to happen!

Tim Haft, CEO, Resume Deli, New York, NY: Try to think of your resume as a living, breathing document that is constantly evolving in tandem with your professional life. Your resume should always be fresh and current and ready to send out at a moment's notice. You never know when opportunity will strike next, and in this day and age you can't afford to be complacent. Update your resume as soon as you land a new job; obtain a degree, certificate, or diploma; achieve a new professional goal; join a professional or trade association; publish an article; make a presentation . . . you get the idea.

Better yet, create what I call a *qualifications bank*. This is simply an exhaustive list of your professional experience, skills, accomplishments, and education. You can organize the contents of your bank chronologically and/or by functional category (for example, communications experience, sales experience, and so on). This bank is strictly for you; no employer need ever see it, so set it up the way that works best for you. You might want to use a spreadsheet or database or simply create a word processing document, but for ease of access, definitely store it electronically.

Every time you accomplish something noteworthy, you will make a "deposit" to your bank. And when it comes time to revise or create a new resume you will be able to do so quite easily by making withdrawals. All the information necessary will be at your fingertips, and it will simply be a question of picking and choosing the right ingredients to make the strongest case possible to an employer.

Lena Bottos: Writing a resume is a daunting task and becomes ever more painful the longer you wait to do it. Dust off your resume after major milestones including additional education, career changes, large projects, or promotions. A good approach is to update your resume immediately after each performance review. That way, you have all your recent accomplishments fresh in your mind.

Updating your resume boosts your focus and confidence, and forces you to think ahead to the next step. It is also much easier to update your resume when you don't need to. If you keep it current, an unexpected job search or interviewing opportunity won't catch you off guard.

We at Salary.com suggest you create a "parking lot" of former resume items rather than permanently deleting them. This way you can easily retrieve those experiences if they would help strengthen your resume for a specific job.

What is the biggest mistake I can make in developing or submitting resumes?

James K. Elkins: The most critical error made in writing resumes is to fail to mention specific accomplishments. Resumes often include excellent job descriptions, but indicate little about how well the job was done. It is very important to include your accomplishments, using data to back them up if possible. It is not sufficient to merely describe a new initiative you introduced, but describe how it benefited the organization in cost savings, product/service improvement, or other tangible ways.

The second major mistake that I see frequently is the use of the functional resume format, where a list of accomplishments is given first. While that approach does highlight achievements, it leaves the employer guessing as to where and when your accomplishments took place. Employers will not spend the time trying to determine sequence and prefer a straightforward chronological approach so that they can see clearly the progression of your career.

Karen S. McAndrew: The biggest mistake you can make in developing your resume is to make it difficult for the reader to find the information relevant to the position he or she is seeking to fill. Typically, the reader will visually scan the resume to determine if the candidate has the required skills and experience for the position. You need to know the requirements of the position and state your qualifications in a way that demonstrates to the reader that you are a good candidate for the position.

Tim Haft: The truth is that there are numerous big mistakes and it's difficult to classify one as the biggest since all of them could result in your resume being tossed in the circular file. That said, here are some definite no-nos:

- Spelling errors or typos. If you can't proofread your own resume, why would an employer trust you on the job?

- Submitting a resume that has streaks, smudges, or is poorly printed. As the saying goes, it's all in the presentation.

- Being dishonest about dates, jobs, grades, or anything else for that matter. If you lie or grossly embellish, the odds are overwhelming that you will get caught, plus it's just plain wrong.

- Missing the target. Your resume must speak to the needs of your target audience. If the first third of your resume isn't relevant to the employer who's reading it, you can kiss your resume good-bye.

· Fluff and jargon. Be clear, direct, and factual with your writing. If you pepper your resume with too many acronyms and empty adjectives you are shooting yourself in the foot.

Dr. Peter A. Manzi: In my twenty years of experience as a career counselor and educator, I have found that not having a specific objective in mind followed by a resume that parallels or reinforces that objective is the single major stumbling block to writing an effective resume. Even if an objective is not stated in the resume itself, it should be apparent in the structure and organization of the resume, and should definitely be stated in the cover letter that goes with it. Oftentimes, as a result of this lack of focus, these resumes come across as weak or unimpressive, with the applicant seeming unsure or indecisive about what he or she wants. It says, "Here I am, tell me what I can do."

The source of this flaw is varied. Some applicants don't want (or know how) to be specific and want an all-purpose resume. For example, I worked with a client with experience in both sales and management in electrical engineering and manufacturing. She tried to use an objective that allowed her to work in sales, management, and research, that is, to open as many doors to employment as possible. She came across as having a few sets of skills and experiences in two of these three areas, but none with depth or a real sense of accomplishment. Her objective (as relayed to me by the CEO of a technical employment firm) was vague and he quickly passed over her resume.

Had she written a resume for sales positions, she could have expanded her sales experience content and included other sales and marketing related experience from other jobs and any relevant college, graduate school, co-op, internship, or even volunteer organization experience. There are many sources of viable skills and experience, and I have found that people tend to underestimate the full range and depth of their skills. A single objective or focused resume requires digging deep into a person's work and educational background and doing a thorough skills assessment. There are a number of self-assessment tools to be found on the Internet, and an applicant can usually get a comprehensive job description from company websites to try to match their skills and achievements with those required in the position sought. Many job search websites contain very brief job descriptions, which is why one should go directly to the HR department of the company.

A good, focused and concise resume requires a lot of think time, decision making, and writing and revision. It is much more time-consuming to construct than a generalist resume. In reality, most people need several different resumes with nonoverlapping objectives as they seek different positions. The lesson here is, there is no shortcut to writing an effective resume. Too much is at stake to be casual or cursory about one's resume.

Laura Hill: Of the potential pitfalls a resume writer may encounter, here are a few:

- Use of first person (*I*).

- Describing accomplishments in a place where the reader can't associate them with the job in which you did them (credibility comes from the context of the job).

- Too-small type size.

- Job descriptions instead of accomplishments.

- Too much fluff before the reader gets to the substance.

- Too much clutter, too many design features, or other attributes that overwhelm the reader's eyes.

- Not targeting the resume to a job function or industry.

- Not including your E-mail address.

Evan Burks: Do not "embellish" your resume. In other words, be honest! Companies are increasing their reliance on background investigations and other techniques to check on your past performance and character. Instead of using your energy in this manner, use it to creatively represent yourself.

Tracy Gartmann: The biggest, most widespread and common mistake you can make is to undersell yourself by not describing your experiences both specifically and quantitatively. Using generic and generalized statements like "Provided child care" communicates very little about you to the reader of your resume. What sorts of child care did you provide? What were you actually doing? You have the ability to set yourself apart from others in each descriptive statement you make, and you must take this opportunity. A more specific and quantitative set of statements would be, "Mentored 45 children ages 7 to 10 in after-school program. Organized and supervised arts and crafts activities that developed and cultivated social, emotional, and creative skills in each child. Coordinated and encouraged good physical health and sportsmanship by leading exercise activities for 45 minutes each day. Ensured safety of each child present." Prioritize your statements so that your most important accomplishments are listed first.

Whenever possible, be results oriented and benefit oriented. How did your performance at your job benefit your employer? Answering this question will set your resume apart, because this is often the weakest element of your competition's resume.

What are some mistakes to avoid?

Dr. Joan Baum: Don't download a resume from the Internet or blindly copy anyone else's look. You will be restricted by someone else's arrangement and not have a place or sufficient place to put in special items. Design your own resume. It's worth the effort. And don't overdo the fonts and type size. As a rule, don't use more than three different formatting features. You want to be readable and neat, not cute and gimmicky.

Don't put down that you type XX wpm. If you're asked, of course do so, but otherwise, don't typecast yourself—pun intended.

If you have a telephone message on your phone that is anything but professional, change it immediately.

Laura Hill: A few of my biggest pet peeves (from the recipient's perspective):

- Sending your resume to any and all jobs irrespective of the fit. When responding to job postings or ads you should only send your resume if your background closely fits the description.

- Making it obvious that the recipient is part of a mass mailing.

- Trying to go around the person designated to recruit for the position.

- Being too pushy: calling too often, calling when posting says "No calls please."

- Mailing it instead of E-mailing it (the latter enables the recipient to save it and access it electronically).

How do you make your resume stand out?

Lena Bottos: It's easy to follow the herd and use word processing or resume writing templates to write a resume. When every candidate ends up using the same format, recruiters and human resources departments have a hard time finding the candidate's personality in the resume. Be original and design a resume that reflects your personality and work style. This is your first presentation of work to a potential employer and it represents the quality and originality of the work they can expect to see in the future.

This is not an arts and crafts project. Keep it clean, crisp, and neat. Save your smiley face icons for your E-mail; do not use them for bullets. You can sparingly use lines, margins, fonts, and font effects to differentiate your resume and focus the reader's attention on the most important text on the page.

Put the most important and applicable facts at the top. The most important thing about yourself that makes you a good candidate for the position should be in the top half of the page. Once you've been identified as a qualified candidate, the rest of your resume comes into play. The reality of it is, when there are many candidates to sift through, even a single page resume may not get enough time for a full read-through. In these cases, the reader will look for phrases or words that immediately stand out as positive or necessary qualities for the position in question. You have to get the reader's attention first.

Use action words that convey your participation and role in the various parts of your experience that you highlight. Speak in terms of accomplishments and achievements. Quantify results when possible. Vary font effects to call the reader's attention to the most important facts. Use bolding, italicizing, underlining, and capitalizing to highlight areas of interest, but don't overdo it. Make sure the end result is clear and organized, not busy.

When you think your resume is complete, print it out and have multiple friends read it. Ask each one what three things in your resume stuck out. Most likely, these are the first three qualities about yourself that will catch your potential employer's eye. If you've structured your resume right, these should be the qualities that make you the person for the job.

Bill Coleman: There are two moments you want your resume to shine. First, you want your resume to stand out at representing a qualified candidate when it's being quickly scanned to determine if it should be in the read pile or the file pile. You want it to be in the read pile. Second, you want the content in your resume to stand out when it is actually being read and compared with other qualified candidates.

To stand out for the first cut in the filtering process, you want your resume to be professional and to demonstrate that you meet the top three most important requirements for the job. Whether it's your most recent job title, career objective, a prior employer, specific experience, or something else, make sure it practically jumps off the page. As journalists say, "don't bury the lead." Use bolding and italics appropriately, and be sure to place those key accomplishments at the top of their respective lists.

When everything in your resume is being read, it is important that the whole document supports you as a strong candidate for the job. Your resume will stand out if it includes items that relate directly to the employer's requirements. Don't forget, your resume can—and should—change for most employment opportunities. Making your resume a perfect match is one of the best ways to make it stand out.

What can you put on your resume to boost your worth?

Bill Coleman: There are several things you can put on your resume—and discuss in your interviews—that can help boost your worth. Actually, they don't help boost your worth; they help prove you're worth more than the average person applying for the job.

Simply put, anything that positions you as a top performer in your job or describes situations in which you performed above the level of your job will help increase your market value. For example, effectively managing people is often a valuable trait. If you have managed more than the typical number of people for your position and/or have some demonstrable superior skills, show that in your resume. If you have ancillary experience beyond the standard job responsibilities, those should be called out. Employers will often pay more for a person they believe has proven the ability to achieve critical results, whatever those may be for the job.

Simple advice:

- Check your spelling again. (Spelling mistakes send a bad signal to a potential employer. Some people won't even consider a resume with a typo.)

- Verify your name, phone number, and E-mail address. (These are the most likely places for typos because everyone assumes they're correct.)

- If you're sending a resume based on a referral, mention the name of the person who referred you in the first sentence of the cover letter. (Make sure the person who receives your cover letter sees the name of his or her colleague so you're more likely to be considered.)

- Say what you did, not what you were "responsible for." (The action sounds better and demonstrates that you've accomplished things.)

- Give results when appropriate—for example, "this project saved the company $50,000," or "this report was used as a model for future engagements." (Quantifying what you've done makes it real, believable, and more memorable.)

- Don't lie.

- Have something in your resume that is uncommon, yet isn't weird. Something to remember you by. (If you sing in a choir, put that under Interests. It will help employers to distinguish you. They'll refer to you as "the singer.")

- Your resume and cover letter are your marketing materials—use them to promote yourself. (If something isn't going to help you get the job, don't include it.)

- Use a permanent E-mail address or a permanent E-mail forwarding address. (This will give your resume a longer shelf life because it will always have up-to-date contact information.)

How much can you ask for?

Lena Bottos: Often, a candidate is asked to put salary expectations in a cover letter. When you are starting a new career or have been out of work for a while you may have no feel for what a fair salary is for the position you are interested in. If you know people in the business, ask them what kind of starting salary you can expect. In addition, there are resources at your disposal to help you. You can use Salary.com's Personal Salary Report to find out what an appropriate salary range is for someone with your background. The worst thing you can do is price yourself out of the job or out of a fair salary before your resume has ever been read.

You can ask for more money if you can support the claim that you're worth it. To do that you need to understand the value of your skills, experiences, and education to the specific employer. If you know specifically what the employer values in an employee filling your desired job, be sure to highlight how you match those valuable skills. Highlight it in your cover letter, in your resume, and most importantly, in your interviews.

When people talk about "how much" they normally are thinking about base pay. If you find that you cannot ask for as much as you think you deserve because the company won't pay that, or doesn't value your experience the same way you do, then it's time to "think outside the box." Concede the lower salary and consider asking for a salary review in three or six months. Another approach is to ask for a signing bonus, which is sometimes a way of increasing a total pay package without upsetting the company's fixed salary structure. Additional stock options, vacation time, and bonus opportunity are also vehicles to help you get to the total compensation you deserve.

Should I always include a cover letter when submitting a resume?

Lena Bottos: Yes. The cover letter is a prologue to your resume. It introduces the reader to you and gives you a voice not inherently communicated in a typical resume. It also sets the bar for your ability to communicate in a business environment. If you are sending your resume to a friend, you may be inclined, or even told, not to bother with a cover letter. Keep in mind that the resume will then be sent to the appropriate parties and your acquaintance is now speaking on your behalf. Take control of the situation and speak for yourself. Who better than you to adequately describe who you are and what you are looking for?

Remember, if you E-mail your resume, the text of the E-mail is your cover letter. Treat it as such, even if you're "just E-mailing it to a friend."

Always assume your E-mail will be forwarded. Don't be cute. Don't be too casual. Do, however, make it clear that you are friends with the person you are E-mailing, because whomever he or she sends the E-mail to will be more likely to consider the resume of the sender's friend.

How formal should I be in writing a cover letter?

Lena Bottos: This depends somewhat on your relationship to the recipient reading the cover letter. If you do not know the person who is receiving your cover letter, you should be formal. This will convey to a potential employer your business etiquette. If you are familiar with the person receiving the cover letter, you should still structure the cover letter formally. You may address the individual less formally and you may be a little more relaxed in the tone of your letter, but keep in mind usually more than one person makes a hiring decision. Your cover letter may be attached with your resume and distributed to other people in the organization. Do not use the cover letter to discuss personal issues that you do not want shared with individuals you do not know and that may have hiring authority.

What is the biggest mistake to avoid in developing my cover letter?

Dr. Janet Scarborough: Many candidates make the mistake of writing vague generalities that fail to convince the prospective employer that there is a good fit between the job seeker's qualifications and the hiring needs of the organization. From a hiring manager perspective, employers want to know how adding you to existing staff will make their work lives easier. They are less interested in facts such as your desire to find "challenging work in a dynamic company" because this statement doesn't say anything. Of course you don't want "boring work in a stagnant company"!

Every job seeker should imagine himself or herself as an employer to visualize what the organization needs to be comfortable with a hiring decision. Don't be afraid to let a little personality and creativity show through, but more importantly, be clear and thorough in demonstrating how your skills and goals are a great match with the requirements of the position being sought.

What is the biggest advantage of posting my resume electronically?

Liz Ryan: It is essential to do this, as it makes it easier for employers or search people to move your resume around and to reference it from anywhere they may be. Although there are many places to post your resume online, one particularly good place is with WorldWIT, the global online community for women (although men are welcome to post resumes there, too) at worldwit.org.

Karen S. McAndrew: The biggest advantage of posting your resume electronically is the potential for it to be seen by large numbers of employers seeking skills that you possess. However, it is imperative that your resume contain "keywords" relevant to the positions you are seeking in order for your resume to gain visibility.

Joseph Terach: Far and away, the greatest advantage of posting your resume electronically to one or more job search websites is the wide exposure it will receive. Few people are aware that there are literally hundreds of job search sites on the Web. Some, such as Career Builder (careerbuilder.com) and Monster (monster.com), cater to the vast majority of job seekers, while others target specific industries or geographic areas.

Posting your resume to tens of job search sites sounds like a daunting task, but online services such as Resume Rabbit (resumerabbit.com) help job seekers to "hop to it" by posting their resumes to multiple job search sites in one fell swoop.

That's the upside. The downside of an online job search is that you do not get to fully target your resume and cover letter, because you never know who's on the receiving end. And creating a more generic resume is a sure way to sell yourself short. So, as easy as electronic posting can be, you don't want to fall into the trap of using this method exclusively. Be sure to complement your online job search by making personal contacts, networking, and using a targeted resume to apply for specific jobs of interest.

Evan Burks: With the advent of the Internet and electronic job boards, the biggest advantage of posting your resume relates to the mass exposure you might receive from hiring companies. There's also a big disadvantage, however. This is simply not the most effective way to pinpoint—or personalize—your job search.

If I plan to submit a resume electronically, should I take any special formatting measures?

Evan Burks: Yes. Don't paste your resume into the body of your E-mail; there's an excellent chance that it will come out looking very different when it reaches the reviewer. Lines could be broken, spacing could be completely different, and so on. Instead, send it as a file attachment, so you can be sure that the reviewer will see it exactly as you sent it. You may also be asked to paste a plain-text version of your resume into the body of an E-mail (see Part I for more on electronic resumes).

What is a portfolio?

Tanya K. Bodzin: A portfolio is a physical or electronic file that you maintain of your accomplishments: ongoing and special projects, assignments, projects done outside of work that showcase your technical expertise or managerial and/or executive expertise. You may want to call it your brag file! Whatever you call it, you need to have one. At the end of the week or a few days think back to determine where did you make a difference, where did you take the lead on a project, where did you contribute to the organization that had a impact. Write it up in the *PAR* format. The PAR format is a description of the *problem*, the *action* you took, and the *results*. Length is not an issue here. The idea is to write up the accomplishment in language that is descriptive so that someone not in your field will understand what you did and its importance.

After four months you will have multiple accomplishments in your portfolio that you can use to update your resume. In addition you can use it as a tool for performance review. Write up your accomplishments before your review and give them to your supervisor. You will have (1) shown that you are a team player, (2) made the supervisor's job easier by jogging his or her memory as to what you really have done this year, (3) increased your own self-esteem by verifying the many things you have done, and (4) created a history that you can call on to update your resume. In most instances when employees use this strategy they are writing their own performance review. What could be better?

What is a good source of background information on career options?

Tracy Gartmann: One of the most helpful tools with regard to career planning and research is the U.S. Department of Labor, Bureau of Labor Statistics *Occupational Outlook Handbook.* Commonly referred to as the *OOH*, this resource is online at bls.gov/oco/home.htm. It lists every job and every industry in the United States, with complete articles about what workers do on the job, working conditions, the training and education needed, earnings, and expected job prospects. It lists professional organizations associated with particular jobs as well, which often have websites and electronic employment listings. In early 2003 the entire website received a facelift that made it not only profoundly useful, but also appealing.

What is the single most important quality of an effective resume?

Susan W. Miller: Most important, the resume should be an effective sales tool for the particular job you are pursuing. The resume is not an application form. The most impressive information about you or what qualifies you most for the job should be at the top of the page. You might consider using an objective, which should be the job title of the position you are pursuing, as well as a summary or qualifications statement. In the body of the resume, use action verbs in the present tense emphasizing skills and accomplishments and the nature and scope of what you have done. Do not put your dates in the margin. They are not what you want to emphasize.

You can include them after the city and state where the company is located. For resumes that will be scanned into a computerized applicant retrieval system, commonly used in larger companies, you should not underline or use fancy graphics, colored paper, or elaborate fonts. Use terms and jargon often used in your field and a resume format that is commonly used in your field.

Dr. Joan Baum: Readability is the most important quality of an effective resume. A resume should be formatted in such a way that it invites a prospective employer to read on, and the content should be itemized as bullets, each item leading off with a dynamic verb that is specific and action oriented so that at a glance, within three seconds, the employer will have an immediate sense of what you have done and what you know. If the resume is readable in these two areas, the employer will be motivated to take a closer look. If the resume is not readable in these two areas, most likely it will be filed you know where.

Gail Liebhaber, Director of Career Services, Harvard Divinity School, Cambridge, MA: Principle, yourcareerdirection.com: It is vitally important that the resume speak to an employer's needs, not the job seeker's. Employers are not usually interested in the fact that you are looking for a challenge or the next step in your career. Instead, they want to know how you can help them solve their problem. After all, if they didn't have a problem they would not be hiring. So find out what they are looking for as best you can by doing your research, and give examples by accomplishments throughout your resume that demonstrate that you are the best person for their organization.

Constance Stevens, Master Career, Career Paths, Davis, CA: I think the most important quality of an effective resume is to have the resume focused on the reader and the specific position. Your resume should answer the question, "Why should we hire you?" It should highlight those skills, experiences, and training/education that you have that are most pertinent to the reader and for that particular job. The concept of a generic resume is obsolete today. Each and every resume you send out needs to be tailored to the reader. That means you'll need to reevaluate your resume and your marketing approach each time. You may need to rewrite sections, edit the order of your resume, or add new information. You need to ask yourself, "Who is reading my resume and what do I want to tell them?"

Part III

Cover Letters and References

Once your resume has been assembled, laid out, and printed to your satisfaction, the next and final step before distribution is to write your cover letter. Though there may be instances where you deliver your resume in person, you will usually send it through the mail or online. Resumes sent through the mail always need an accompanying letter that briefly introduces you and your resume. The purpose of the cover letter is to get a potential employer to read your resume, just as the purpose of the resume is to get that same potential employer to call you for an interview.

Like your resume, your cover letter should be clean, neat, and direct. A cover letter usually includes the following information:

1. Your name and address (unless it already appears on your personal letterhead) and your phone number(s); see item 7.

2. The date.

3. The name and address of the person and company to whom you are sending your resume.

4. The salutation ("Dear Mr." or "Dear Ms." followed by the person's last name, or "To Whom It May Concern" if you are answering a blind ad).

5. An opening paragraph explaining why you are writing (for example, in response to an ad, as a follow-up to a previous meeting, at the suggestion of someone you both know) and indicating that you are interested in whatever job is being offered.

6. One or more paragraphs that tell why you want to work for the company and what qualifications and experiences you can bring to the position. This is a good place to mention some detail about that particular company that makes you want to work there; this shows that you have done some research before applying.

7. A final paragraph that closes the letter and invites the reviewer to contact you for an interview. This can be a good place to tell the potential employer which method would be best to use when contacting you. Be sure to give the correct phone number and a good time to reach you, if that is important. You may mention here that your references are available upon request.

8. The closing ("Sincerely" or "Yours truly") followed by your signature in a dark ink, with your name typed under it.

Your cover letter should include all of this information and be no longer than one page in length. The language used should be polite, businesslike, and to the point. Don't attempt to tell your life story in the cover letter; a long and cluttered letter will serve only to annoy the reader. Remember that you need to mention only a few of your accomplishments and skills in the cover letter. The rest of your information is available in your resume. If your cover letter is a success, your resume will be read and all pertinent information reviewed by your prospective employer.

PRODUCING THE COVER LETTER

Cover letters should always be individualized because they are always written to specific individuals and companies. Never use a form letter for your cover letter or copy it as you would a resume. Each cover letter should be unique, and as personal and lively as possible. (Of course, once you have written and rewritten your first cover letter until you are satisfied with it, you can certainly use similar working in subsequent letters. You may want to save a template on your computer for future reference.) Keep a hard copy of each cover letter so you know exactly what you wrote in each one. Remember that every letter is unique and depends on the particular circumstances of the individual writing it and the job for which he or she is applying.

After you have written your cover letter, proofread it as thoroughly as you did your resume. Again, spelling or punctuation errors are a sure sign of carelessness, and you don't want that to be a part of your first impression on a prospective employer. This is no time to trust your spellcheck function. Even after going through a spelling and grammar check, your cover letter should be carefully proofread by at least one other person.

Print the cover letter on the same quality bond paper you used for your resume. Remember to sign it, using a good dark-ink pen. Handle the letter and resume carefully to avoid smudging or wrinkling, and mail them together in an appropriately sized envelope. Many stores sell matching envelopes to coordinate with your choice of bond paper.

Keep an accurate record of all resumes you send out and the results of each mailing. This record can be kept on your computer, in a calendar or notebook, or on file cards. Knowing when a resume is likely to have been received will keep you on track as you make follow-up phone calls.

About a week after mailing resumes and cover letters to potential employers, contact them by telephone. Confirm that your resume arrived and ask whether an interview might be possible. Be sure to record the name of the person you spoke to and any other information you gleaned from the conversation. It is wise to treat the person answering the phone with a great deal of respect; sometimes the assistant or receptionist has the ear of the person doing the hiring.

EIGHT KEY POINTS

Keep the following eight points in mind when writing your cover letters:

1. Address your cover letter to a specific person. This should be the person most likely to hire you. You can call the company where you wish to work and ask for the person's name.

2. Make sure you tell the employer exactly what job you are applying for and, if it was announced in the want ads or some other place, how you heard about it.

3. Let the employer see that you know something about the company (what the company does and how you can contribute).

4. Be enthusiastic in your letter without overdoing it.

5. Tell the employer about one outstanding quality you have and how it relates to the job you want. This could be in addition to what appears on your resume.

6. Be brief and businesslike. Be sure that your typed cover letter is picture-perfect with no errors.

7. Let employers know that you will contact them within several days. (A week after you send your letter and resume is usually a good amount of time.)

8. Do not send photocopies of your cover letters. You must send an original letter to each employer. The letter should be typed (word processed) on the same kind of paper as the resume.

Here are two sample cover letters. The first example accompanies a resume sent in response to an advertised job opening. The second example is an inquiry letter accompanying a resume and sent to inquire about possible openings.

Response to an Advertised Job Opening

901 East Main Street   August 25, 2003
Rochester, NY 14623
(585) 555-4402 (cell)

Allied Home Services
Attn: Ms. Cynthia Jones
4742 Graham Avenue
Rochester, NY 14623

Dear Ms. Jones:

I wish to be considered for the position of Team Leader as advertised on your company's website. My varied experience, language skills (English, French, and Spanish), and ability to work well with and supervise others would be of great benefit to a company such as yours.

I look forward to meeting you and will call next Monday to arrange an interview. Thank you for your consideration.

Very truly yours,

Maria Delas

Inquiry About Possible Openings

Mary Field
2012 Front Street • Hickory, NC 28602 • 828-555-5289 (cell)

May 2, 2003

Ms. Smith
Human Resources Department
X Appliance Company
491 Charles Street
Hickory, NC 28602

Dear Ms. Smith:

A notice of the forthcoming opening of X Appliance Store at the West Hickory Shopping Center in July recently caught my attention. My interest is both as a customer (an appliance store specializing in ranges and microwaves will be a welcome addition in this part of the city) and as a potential employee (I have targeted appliance demonstration and sales as my primary occupational objective). There are many reasons why I am qualified to work for X Appliance Company, including:

• Seven years experience in appliance demonstration/sales.
• Experience teaching microwave cooking classes.
• Supervisory experience.

My previous employment with the Carolina Appliance Company involved demonstrating new stoves to individual consumers and managers of retail outlets. This experience provided me the opportunity to develop techniques that subsequently improved sales 15 percent in a one-year period. In turn, the company honored me for this achievement.

As you know, microwave cooking is an important method of meal preparation in more than 80 percent of American homes. I have become adept at using mine both for my family and in preparing classes for our local Adult Education Center. In addition, I've developed a microwave cookbook for my students and am enclosing my favorite chicken recipe, which I hope you will also enjoy.

I strongly feel that my unique background in both sales and continuing education in management and current business practices with the Home Economics in Business Association would be a useful addition to your sales force. I'll call this week in hopes that we can arrange a meeting to discuss any possibilities with your firm. Thank you so much for your consideration.

Sincerely,

Mary Field

enclosure

Response to an Advertised Job Opening

Alice Jensen
524 Avery Lane ✦ Tulsa, Oklahoma 59304 ✦ 918-555-5234 (cell)

Ms. Jones   October 3, 2003
Human Resources Director
ABC Inc.
1857 N. Cleveland Street
Tulsa, OK 52124

Dear Ms. Jones:

I am writing in response to your ad for an office clerk in the *Tulsa Times* on September 30. 1 have spent considerable time researching your company and I feel that ABC Inc. would be the perfect work environment for me to demonstrate my skills and abilities. The fact that ABC Inc. is a small but rapidly expanding company presents some interesting challenges and opportunities in which I'm eager to take part.

Your ad stated that ABC Inc. is looking for someone with experience in general office skills. I have been involved in this line of work for many years through volunteer and paid positions and have honed my skills in typing, budgeting, filing, answering telephones and correspondence, greeting customers, and running standard office equipment. In addition, I'm proficient in the Microsoft Office suite and am completely comfortable with new technologies. Specifically, I have considerable experience in the following:

✦ preparing business correspondence (90 wpm)
✦ creating statistical and financial reports
✦ processing inventory and tax forms
✦ writing activity bulletins and newsletters
✦ maintaining filing systems for several organizations, including a 300+ client database

In addition to my considerable work experience in office management, I have successfully completed several administrative training courses at Tulsa Community College. I am very familiar with the business world, work well in both group and individual situations, and am eager to take on new tasks and experiences. I work well under pressure and am adept at meeting deadlines.

I understand that, for a growing company such as ABC Inc., efficiency is very important, and I believe that I could make a contribution to ABC Inc. by increasing efficiency in the office. I will call you at the end of the week to schedule a convenient time to discuss more about the possibility of my working for ABC Inc. Thank you for your consideration.

Sincerely,

Alice Jensen

REFERENCES

Often a job listing asks for one or more letters of recommendation, or for references. The following suggestions will help you request a reference from anyone:

1. Choose a person who knows your abilities. Ask people ahead of time if you may use them as references or if they will write a letter of recommendation.

2. If possible, make an appointment to ask the person to write the letter of recommendation. Allow ten to fourteen days for the completion of the letter.

3. If it is not possible to meet with the person, telephone to ask permission to use him or her as a reference, and follow up with a letter.

4. Give the person a stamped envelope addressed to the employer, a copy of the job listing, a statement about your strengths and skills, and a copy of your resume.

5. Write a short thank-you note to each person who helped you.

Now that you've carefully prepared them, you should make a great impression with the strong, straightforward resume and personalized cover letter you have just created.

Part IV

Sample Resumes

The sample resumes presented in this part are based on actual resumes prepared with the help of practicing librarians. Each has been used successfully by the type of job seeker described before each sample. No one resume will fit your situation exactly, but one or several studied together may give you the ideas you need to design your own resume. At the end of this part, there are several resumes in Spanish for Spanish speakers who are applying for jobs in a Spanish-speaking setting.

WOMAN RETURNING TO WORK

A woman reentering the workplace after an extended period away from the job market must convince a prospective employer that she has skills that she acquired as a homemaker and participant in community affairs.

Some women tend to belittle their jobs as full-time homemakers and see little relationship between the home and the paid workplace. But keep in mind that daily activities such as time and money management, organization of schedules, teaching, nutrition, and many more jobs are marketable skills. An unpaid job does not mean that the job does not require competence. It takes as much skill to work in a volunteer position as in a paid one.

A functional resume will emphasize the skills used as homemaker or volunteer. Recent and important activities can be stressed, and employment gaps will not be as evident. Do not list personal information such as age, health, marital status, or number of children.

Decide what skills to include in your resume—usually those dealing with data, people, and things—then choose those you wish to emphasize. List the most important ones first, using language of the field to which you are applying. (Reading newspaper ads, websites, and trade publications can help you identify the proper language.) In listing your skills, there is no need to distinguish those used in unpaid from those used in paid experience.

Woman Returning to Work

Yetta Lewin

3122 High Road
Warwick, RI 02888
(401) 555-7766
Yetta_Lewin@xxx.com

Education
J.D., Harvard Law School, 1998
Graduated top 10%

Skills
Raised four children:
- Developed tolerance, patience, and negotiating skills.
- Learned to develop strategies to achieve goals.
- Exercised sound judgment in all areas of child rearing.
- Developed useful time-management skills.

As wife to the city comptroller, I accomplished the following:
- Created a foundation that funded three arts centers for the handicapped.
- Established a volunteer theater program in Warwick General Hospital.
- Gained financial assistance for breast cancer support organization.
- Founded the Warwick, RI, division of The Breast Cancer Coalition.
- Organized funding activities for the Coalition.
- Instituted a yearly walk-a-thon for the Susan G. Komen Breast Cancer Foundation.

Registration
Member of the Bar Association. Licensed to practice in Rhode Island and Massachusetts.

Woman Returning to Work

MIA MERRIWEATHER

20 Cedar Pines Lane • Logan, Utah 84322 • (801) 555-2956

OBJECTIVE
To return to a challenging position as a music therapist.

EDUCATION
Utah State University, Logan, Utah
Bachelor of Science Degree in Recreation Therapy, 1998

VOLUNTEER EXPERIENCE
2000–present
➤ Assisted in the affairs of the Navajo Economic Opportunity Bureau.
➤ Established a local community development program.
➤ Designed projects to improve housing conditions and availability.
➤ Developed strategies and campaigned to increase funding for medical care and educational facilities.
➤ Lobbied and achieved funding for a community-based alcoholism treatment program.
➤ Worked directly with Navajo youth, enrolling them in counseling and job training programs.
➤ Promoted a successful food drive for the Navajo community.

PROFESSIONAL EXPERIENCE
Salt Lake Rehabilitation Center, Salt Lake City, Utah
Recreational Therapist, 1999–2000
➤ Sought to reverse the negative effects of disabilities by building self-esteem through various activities.
➤ Developed individual treatment plans.
➤ Organized and coordinated a yearly arts fair in which all clients participated.
➤ Presented four plays a year in the community theater. Acting and backstage activities conducted solely by our clients.
➤ Supervised three recreational therapists in charge of scheduling board game and sports events.
➤ Supervised two therapists who managed the leisure activities program.
➤ Encouraged family members to participate in treatment.
➤ Received Mayor's Award for Achievement in the area of Community Service, 1990 and 1991.

References available on request

Woman Returning to Work

MARY NUSSBAUM

153 Main Street

Flushing, NY 11367

Home: (718) 555-5411

Pager: (718) 555-7990

CAREER OBJECTIVE

To secure employment as a travel consultant in an agency that offers advancement opportunities.

ACTIVITIES

Homemaker   Dec. 2001–present

Five years experience raising triplets.

* Organized and managed daily routines.
* Scheduled educational and play activities.
* Prepared meals.
* Studied numerous psychology books.
* Developed patience, insight, and understanding.

EMPLOYMENT HISTORY

Travel Consultant   Aug. 1999–2001

F.L.Y. Travel Agency, New York, NY

* Arranged conventions for major corporations.
* Organized entertainment and recreational activities.
* Planned sightseeing trips.
* Negotiated with hotels for group room and meal rates.
* Prepared efficient and economical business travel plans.

Reservation Specialist   July 1992–Aug. 1999

TWA Airlines, Peoria, IL

* Handled customer requests using World Span computer system.
* Arranged hotel and car rental accommodations.
* Computed fares.
* Resolved disputes.

EDUCATION

B.A. Psychology, Rockford College, 1992

FOREIGN LANGUAGES

Hebrew, French

REFERENCES

Available on request.

Woman Returning to Work

Joan Jackson

258 Old Farm Road • Dublin, OH 43217
614-555-0961 • JoanJackson21@xxx.net

Management/Organization

— Managed "Friends of the Library" Bookstore and Special Booksales, raising
  $7,500 annually
— Coordinated TWIGS Christmas Bazaar that made a profit of $15,000
— Served as President of School Parent/Teacher Association
— Organized Statewide Girl Scout Weekend Jamboree for 1,500 scouts

Teaching/Training

— Tutored English as a Second Language student for four years
— Served as docent for library tours for schoolchildren
— Acted as Room Mother to aid classroom teacher
— Conducted workshops for tutors for adult new readers
— Worked as Girl Scout Troop Leader for three years

Work History

1995–Present	— Volunteer with Public Library of Columbus and Franklin County, Columbus
	— Literacy Council, Dublin Public Schools, Girl Scouts of America, TWIGS, and other community associations
1993–1995	— Caseworker, Franklin County Human Services Department
	— Provided counseling for families needing public assistance
1993–1995	— Library Assistant, Bexley Public Library
	— Provided reader's advisory and reference help to library patrons

Education

1992	B.A. Sociology, Ohio University
1990	Courses at Franklin University in Introduction to Microcomputers, Word Processing, and File Management

References furnished on request

SKILLED TRADESPERSON

If you are a tradesperson, the employer is interested in what you can do. Your resume should tell an employer all the skills that you have. The types of machines that you can operate show that you can learn to operate others. It is also important that you tell about the special licenses that you have.

If the occupation has a union, be sure to list the type and length of your apprenticeship. How long you have been a journeyman and what kinds of supervisory experience you have are also important. The types and length of schooling and a journeyman's card can help to get the job.

In the third of the following three resume examples, the employer can see that Caldwell has worked for the same company for a significant amount of time. This indicates to the employer that the applicant must have showed up for work and produced satisfactory results. In your resume be sure to list the companies that you have worked for and approximately how long.

Remember, do not list personal information such as age, health, marital status, or number of children.

Skilled Tradesperson

MIKE BOYLE

288 PALISADE AVENUE
JERSEY CITY, NEW JERSEY 07306
201-555-2938

Job Desired

Apprentice mechanic with automotive repair company with opportunity to train as auto mechanic.

Education

Dickinson High School, Jersey City, 1999–present
Hudson Regional Junior-Senior High School, Highlands, NJ, 1994–1996

Skills

Mechanically inclined with skills ranging from basic auto mechanics to very technical electrical diagnostics.

Work Experience

Dickinson High School Auto Shop, 2000–present
Duties: Tune-ups, oil changes, general checkup and troubleshooting in student-run auto mechanics shop. Diagnose and repair mechanical problems on cars, trucks, and vans.

East Jersey Radiator, 2000–present
Duties: Cleaning and testing radiators, installing replacement radiators, and motor detailing. Shop services both foreign and domestic cars. Assisted with stock warehouse.

Northern Landscape Maintenance, 1999–2000
Duties: Planting, mowing, pruning, and hedging for three apartment complexes and four office complexes. Responsible for maintaining nursery inventory.

References

Available upon request.

Skilled Tradesperson

JUAN SANCHEZ

3838 16th Street
San Bernardino, CA 92401
(714) 555-6155

OBJECTIVE
Responsible position requiring proven mechanical skills.

ACHIEVEMENTS
◆ Provided comprehensive mechanical services for military aircraft.
◆ Received excellent evaluations from superiors.
◆ Earned three promotions in rank based on job accomplishments and overall performance.

WORK EXPERIENCE
United States Coast Guard, 1996–2002
Specialty: Aircraft maintenance and repair
Rating: Aviation Structural Mechanic First Class (E-6)

Responsibilities:
◆ Performed comprehensive duties related to handling, inspecting, servicing, and maintaining aircraft structures and components.
◆ Fabricated and assembled metal parts.
◆ Made repairs.
◆ Performed nondestructive testing.
◆ Painted and maintained painting equipment.
◆ Maintained hydraulic systems, landing gear, fuel tanks, and other components.
◆ Performed related duties.

EDUCATION
Graduate, Aviation Training Technical Center, USCG, Elizabeth City, North Carolina, 1997

Diploma, Warren High School, San Bernardino, California, 1996

Skilled Tradesperson

JOSEPH W. CALDWELL
346 Buena Vista • Pocatello, Idaho 83251
(208) 555-6682 or E-mail: jwc@xxx.com

JOB GOAL
Construction foreman for housing construction company.

SKILLS
Experience in a wide range of construction and wood products occupations. Thorough knowledge of indigenous woods and their suitability for construction. Twenty years of supervisory experience.

WORK HISTORY
Supervisor, Twin Peaks Plywood, Pocatello, ID
Trained and supervised mill workers in all areas of mill operation. Scheduled shifts of 24 workers each, three shifts a day. Worked relief schedule on weekends. Developed safety awareness program. Monitored safety procedures. Consulted with SAIF inspectors for methods of improving working environment safety. Employed continuously from 1988 to present.

Shift Foreman, Idaho Lumber Supply, Boise, ID
Supervised splitters, pullers, and saw operators on day shift. Trained workers in all aspects of lumber mill operation. Monitored safety procedures. Employed initially as mill worker; worked seasonally from 1982 to 1988 (moved).

Carpentry Crewman, Dales Construction, Boise, ID
Worked on carpentry crew building residential dwellings and office complexes in Boise and environs. Experienced with foundation work, roofing, Sheetrocking, and finish carpentry. Worked seasonally from 1979 to 1988 (moved).

Woodworker, Ames Oak Furniture, Boise, ID
Operated lathe, power saw, miter saw, drill press, scroll saw, burnishing sander, and other power equipment in the manufacture and finishing of oak furniture. Employed full-time from 1977 to 1979 (business relocated out of state).

EDUCATION
Boise Central High School, graduated 1977

MEMBERSHIPS
International Mill Workers Local #655; Carpenters Local #2815

Skilled Tradesperson

R O B E R T   W I L C O X

1805 Grayland Avenue   (801) 555-1918 home phone
Price, UT 84501   (801) 555-9089 cell phone

E M P L O Y M E N T   O B J E C T I V E

Position in the telephone, power, or cable industry

R E L A T E D   E X P E R I E N C E

Line Installer and Repairer, U.S. Navy, 1996–2002

Performed a variety of duties involved in installing, maintaining, and repairing electrical cables and communication lines, including:

- Utility pole erection
- Mechanical lift, plow, and other equipment operation
- Overhead communications and electrical cable installation between utility poles
- Installation of street lights and other lighting systems
- Splicing and sealing cables for watertightness
- Installation of voltage regulators, electrical transformers, and voltage regulators
- Related duties

E D U C A T I O N

Completed special training including program in cable splicing and repair at Navy Construction Training Center, Port Hueneme, CA, 1996

WORKER WITH LITTLE TRAINING OR SKILLS

People often forget that they have abilities that can help them get better-paying jobs. Even if they are not trained for a specific trade or profession, these abilities may be job related. Some of these abilities are:

- Being able to speak other languages in addition to English

- Having a valid driver's license

- Getting along well with other people

- Having experience working in groups with children or other adults

- Supervising other people (children or adults)

- Hobbies

- Travel

- Reading books and magazines about the kinds of work that you would like to do

The following resumes were written for people with some work experience but little training. These resumes include skills and other qualifications that were not actually performed on the job. If you lack the skills needed to work in a technical, trade, or professional job, you can still write a resume that will impress an employer. Your other abilities and skills can sometimes indicate strengths that make up, at least in part, for lack of formal training.

Worker with Little Training or Skills

DEBBIE R. NEWELL

2986 Middle Avenue
Rapid City, SC 57701
(605) 555-1307

OBJECTIVE
Full-time employment as a secretary while I attend night classes.

PARTICULARS
- Typing—75 wpm
- WordPerfect, Word
- Lotus, PowerPoint, Quicken

EDUCATION
Rapid City High School, Rapid City, SC
Degree: 2003, General Studies
I will attend Western Dakota Vocational Technical Institute for 2 years beginning in the fall of 2004.

WORK EXPERIENCE
Kmart
Clerk—women's clothing department
Cash Register Operator
9/98 to present
Full-time during the summer
Part-time during the academic year

EXTRACURRICULAR
Member of the high school choir and jazz choir.
Participated in Girl Scout activities for 3 years.
Served as a camp counselor for Brownies and Pixies at the City Park.

REFERENCES
Available upon your request

Worker with Little Training or Skills

GEORGE WEST

1205 ORANGE ROAD • FARMINGDALE, NY 11736 • (516) 555-0020 (CELL)

JOB OBJECTIVE

A position as a mechanic with a major automotive dealership

QUALIFICATIONS AND EXPERIENCE

☆ Maintain very strong interest in automobiles and trucks, and automotive equipment.

☆ Read and study *Automotive Restorer*, *New England Mechanic*, publications of Automotive Service Association, other publications.

☆ Attend automotive trade shows and auctions.

☆ Repair and rebuild cars and trucks.

☆ Completely rebuilt 1994 Chevrolet using old and new parts. I have been using this car regularly for the last five years.

☆ Have frequently advised others on mechanical problems and repair needs.

☆ Have sold automotive parts and supplies.

EMPLOYMENT HISTORY

1996–Present	Self-employed auto mechanic
1992–1996	John Grey's Automotive—Nassau, New York
1993–1996	Dale Mobile
1991–1993	Burger King

EDUCATION

Nassau Community College—BOCES
Equivalency Diploma, 1991
Courses in: Automotive Technology
Electronic Technology
Nassau Vocational High School, 1987–1989
Courses in: Automotive Repair
Body Work
Electronic Assembly

Worker with Little Training or Skills

AMANDA MARTIN
1076 North 27th
Phoenix, Arizona 85028
(602) 555-3874

GOAL   A career in the computer industry.

EDUCATION   Shadow Mountain High School, 1996–2000
                    Cumulative G.P.A.: 3.75
                    Relevant Courses:
                    Computer Science
                    Computer Applications
                    Computer Programming (C++, Visual Basic)
                    Algebra
                    Geometry
                    Trigonometry
                    Precalculus

ACHIEVEMENTS   Worked on five-member team to develop new computer
                    software for grading multiple-choice tests, recording
                    grades, and providing bell curves and other averages
                    that could be used for assigning letter grades.

                    Customized programming software for use by students
                    with visual impairments.

                    Won annual district prize for best computer program-
                    ming solution.

REFERENCES   Available upon request.

Maria Delas

901 East Main Street • Flourville, PA 19701
(215) 555-3132 • (215) 555-1857 (cell)
mdelas@xxx.com

Job Objective

*A position as a supervisor in a professional
cleaning/domestic/housekeeping service.*

Experience

— Supervise others in cleaning residences/commercial offices
— Clean private residences, commercial and professional offices
— Have been employed as exclusive housekeeper

Employment History

2001–Present	Dial-a-Maid Industries
1999–2001	Exclusive Housekeeper for two private residences
1997–2001	Apex Cleaning Service
1996–1997	Self-employed housecleaner

Other Qualifications

— Speak, read, write fluent French, can speak Spanish
— Pennsylvania State Driver's License
— Can be bonded

Education

1992–1996	Santa Rosa Secondary School—Barbados, West Indies

Worker with Little Training or Skills

JOHN NOWARK

217 Arthur Avenue

Omaha, NE 68103

402-555-9818

johnn@xxx.com

Career Goal: To secure a position as an assistant greenskeeper.

Education: Dundee High School Graduate, 2004

General Education
GPA 3.00/4.00 overall, 3.50/4.00 science
Science Classes
Horticulture, 2 semesters

Art Courses
Ceramics, 1 semester
Basic Art, Drawing, 1 semester

Mathematics
Algebra, 2 semesters
Geometry, 2 semesters

Experience: **Summers 2000 to 2003**
Sugar Hill Nursery
453 Eureka Lane, Omaha, NE 69337
Nursery Assistant—Prepared nursery beds for planting; watered, weeded, and sprayed trees, shrubs, and plants; and filled orders.

Summers 2000 to 2002
4-H Camp
1500 Eureka Lane, Omaha, NE 69337
Counselor—Responsible for 20 children each year for one week in the month of July.

References: Available upon request.

Worker with Little Training or Skills

JACKSON GARVEY

1134 N.E. 14th
El Dorado, Kansas 67402
jgarvey@xxx.net

CAREER GOAL

My short-term objective is to obtain a position as a warehouseman. For the long term, my goal is to complete college training in engineering and manufacturing.

EDUCATION

El Dorado High School, McCullom Road, El Dorado
Courses studied: metal shop, computer applications, three years of wood-working, and three-dimensional design.

WORK EXPERIENCE

Warehouse Worker for Gates Tire Company, El Dorado, Kansas
June to August 2000
Assisted with receiving shipments, stocking, and sending shipments. Drove forklift and operated loading dock.

Landscape Maintenance for private individuals
June to August 1999
Planted and removed plants and provided lawn maintenance for a variety of personal clients.

Field Worker for Townsend Farms, Inc., June to August 1998
Planted and harvested several crops for small family farm operation.

SKILLS

Able to operate the following: lathe, table saw, drill press, sander, bench grinder, arc welder, Hyster 2450 forklift.

ACTIVITIES

Junior varsity and varsity baseball and soccer. Member of Greater El Dorado Soccer Club.

REFERENCES

Available on request.

FIRST-TIME JOB SEEKER

The functional resume can be beneficial for first-time job seekers to use, since they may have little work experience. The functional type allows first-time job seekers to stress their capabilities and accomplishments in school activities and in life.

The following resumes show how recent graduates present their qualifications for a job by concentrating on skills they have acquired rather than jobs they have held.

First-Time Job Seeker (High School)

KARIN BOWLES

2050 CROWN BOULEVARD, APT. C • DENVER, CO 80204
(303) 555-2280

GOAL

A career in business administration

EXPERIENCE

LEADERSHIP   As a member of the finance committee for the Associated Students of Kennedy High School, I was responsible for supervising the planning and execution of schoolwide fund-raising projects such as candy sales and the student carnival. I also set meeting dates and presided over meetings, reported to student council, and worked with the student government advisor on budgeting.

COMMUNICATION   Worked on the publicity committee for several student events and election campaigns. Wrote text for fliers and signs and assisted with speech writing. Each campaign ended in election victory for my candidate.

Completed two semesters of business communications courses. Also completed three years of honors-level English composition and three years of French. Have working knowledge of spoken and written French.

ORGANIZATION   Served as assistant librarian, a position usually held by a paid professional, during the semester prior to graduation. Directed a research methods seminar for freshman students. Answered questions about library reference materials and online research sources. Supervised student workers in shelving books. Updated computerized database.

EDUCATION

Kennedy High School
2855 S. Lamar Street
Denver, CO 80227
9/99–6/03
Final G.P.A.: 3.75

Pertinent Courses: Business Law, Accounting, Computer Applications in Business, Office Procedures, Word Processing, Business, Management

First-Time Job Seeker (High School)

Mary Jo Baptiste

2240 N.W. Nebraska Avenue • Washington, D.C. 20016
202-555-7465 • mjb@xxx.com

Objective
To obtain a training position as a preschool guide in a Montessori preschool.

Experience
Parks & Recreation Day Camp Leader, Washington, D.C.
Summer 1999 and 2000.
> Planned programs for children 4-8 years old. Built rapport and communications with parents. Provided supervision of children on play structures during breaks. Taught teamwork skills through problem solving in groups of six children. Taught crafts, songs, and dances. Led storytelling for children aged 10-14.

Outdoor School Counselor and Instructor, D.C. School District, 1998–2000.
> Counseled, supervised, and instructed sixth-grade students from various Washington elementary schools during one-week program each spring. Assumed responsibility for twelve girls. Served as live-in counselor three years, one year as instructor emphasizing environmental education.

Other part-time employment: waitress, housekeeper, clerical assistant.

Educational Background
Coolidge High School, Washington, D.C.
Graduation Date: June 2001

Relevant Courses: Human Development, Childhood Education, Psychology, Sociology, Social Science, Speech and Communications.

Honors: Who's Who Among American High School Students, Future Teachers of America, Volunteer Student Activist of the Year (all-school nomination), District of Columbia Youth of the Month (President's Council on Youth), Quill and Scroll (journalism honor society).

Special Skills and Interests
Reporter on the high school newspaper staff for two years. Published an article in the *Arts Weekly*, Washington, D.C., February 2001. Knowledge of Native American culture, including traditional songs, dances, and crafts.

References are available upon request.

First-Time Job Seeker (College)

Linda J. Lane

10166 N.E. 112th Place • Kirkland, WA 99033
(206) 555-9622 • (206) 555-5332 (cell)
lanelj@xxx.net

JOB OBJECTIVE: Management Trainee Position

EDUCATION: Bachelor of Arts, Business Administration, 2003
                   Washington State University
                   Pullman, Washington
                   Concentration: Management
                   Minor: Management Information Systems

                   MANAGEMENT
                        —Managed sorority house kitchen
                        —Carried full course load
                        —Competed on swim team
                        —Served as sorority business manager
                        —Supervised kitchen ordering

                   ORGANIZATION
                        —Organized and coordinated fund-raising
                          events
                        —Billed members for sorority dues
                        —Inventoried kitchen supplies
                        —Scheduled thirty sorority members for
                          kitchen duty
                        —Completed office tasks—filing, typing, and
                          photocopying

                   COMMUNICATION
                        —Motivated sorority members to meet orga-
                          nizational goals
                        —Prepared monthly financial statements
                        —Wrote column for campus newspaper

WORK EXPERIENCE: Business Manager, Alpha Delta Pi, Washington
                   State University, Pullman, WA, 2002–2003

REFERENCES   Confidential Placement File
                   Washington State University
                   Pullman, WA 99004

MICHAEL TARSUS

798 NINTH STREET • OAKDALE, PA 15189 • (412) 555-8495 • tarsusmb@xxx.com

OBJECTIVE:	**Laboratory Assistant**
EDUCATION:	**B.S. Biology, June 2002** Westminster College, New Wilmington, PA
ACCOMPLISHMENTS:	**Histology Study** • Compared normal organ tissue of rats to tissue of rats given foreign substances • Helped prepare specimens for SEM and TEM microscopes • Observed specimens under microscopes and recorded observations • Trained in Electron Microscopy
EXPERIENCE:	**12/02–Present Physical Therapy Aide** *Harmerville Rehabilitation Center, Harmerville, PA* • Assisted patients with therapeutic exercise • Researched new therapies for spinal cord injury patients **6/02–12/02 Laboratory Proctor** *Westminster College, New Wilmington, PA* • Prepared specimens and solutions for biology lab • Designed lab tests • Supervised lab and assignment reviews
ACTIVITIES:	**Sigma Alpha Fraternity** • Pledge Class President • Pan-Hellenic Chairman • Brother-of-the-Year 2002 • Ambassadors Club

Marylou Bademacher

1414 N. Montebello Drive ✤ Berkeley, CA 98028
415/555-4930 ✤ mloub@xxx.net

Education

University of California at Berkeley
Bachelor of Science in Business
Expected June 2001

Honors

Beta Gamma Upsilon Honorary Society
Dean's List
Manley Writing Award, 1999

Activities

Treasurer, Gamma Gamma Gamma Society
Freshman Advisor
Homecoming Planning Committee
Alumni Welcoming Committee

Work Experience

AT&T, New York, NY
Marketing Intern, 2000
✤ Assisted marketing staff in the areas of research, demographics, sales
forecasts, identifying new customers, and Internet promotion.

University of California at Berkeley
Office Assistant, Journalism School, 1998–2000
✤ Assisted with registrations, filing, and typing. Arranged application
materials. Assembled course packs.

Special Skills

Fluent in German. Hands-on computer experience using Microsoft
Office 2000.

CAREER CHANGER

Changing careers in today's work world is not unusual. Some people change jobs as many as eight times during their working lives and may also change careers as many as three times or more.

Some people change careers because they wind up in the wrong job or find dissatisfaction in their job. Others change because they are unable to keep up with new technology. Still others are forced into career changes because they have reached a dead end in their career or had to move to a location where there are no jobs available in their chosen career. You may find that your interests and needs have changed and, therefore, you too must change careers.

Whatever your reasons are for changing your career, there are some things you must think about when you choose your new career and begin to prepare your resume. First, you must evaluate your skills, abilities, education, and experience in relation to your new career choice. Can you match those elements with the minimum qualifications you will need in your new job? Second, are there enough jobs available so that you are not locked out of your new career? Next, you should learn what the outlook is for that career. Will there still be jobs available five or ten years from now? Are there opportunities for advancement, or will you hit another dead end after a few years in your new career?

Once you have given some thought to these things and are still determined to go ahead with your career change, you must prepare a resume that will market those skills and others that are transferable to your new career. You may have also acquired new skills through education and independent learning that directly relate to your new career choice. Such information is important to include in your resume. In these cases, the best resume format to use is the functional or skills-based resume. This format allows you to highlight your transferable skills, knowledge, and other related experience.

For example, you might be a librarian with many years of experience and you wish to go back into the field in which you were originally interested—political science. A realistic option for you might be to pursue a career as a professional political campaign or party manager. Much of the managerial, supervisory, and research experience gained as a librarian can certainly be utilized in the political arena. Further, your educational background and some of your early professional experience can be directly related to your new career choice. (See the following example for Katherine Hayes.)

Another example: A former drafter has lost his position due to downsizing. He has tired of this career area, and has trouble keeping up with changes brought into the drafting industry by increasing computerization. However, his experience as a home owner and self-styled real estate expert led to completion of a real estate sales course and licensing exam. Now he is prepared to assume an entry-level sales position in the real estate industry. By doing his homework, this soon-to-be real estate tycoon learned that property is still the safest investment and that more and more people will be buying and selling property in the coming decades. By emphasizing his interests and recent training, this former drafter should have no trouble finding a sales position. (See the sample resume for Douglas Adams.)

Career Changer

Katherine Hayes

5301 Forest Park
Chula Vista, California 91910

(619) 555-2428 (cell)
Kathybhayes@xxx.com

Objective

Political campaign or party management

SUMMARY OF QUALIFICATIONS

15 years managerial and supervisory work in public service
— Project design and administration
— Staff recruitment, training, and supervision
— Public and media relations
— Sophisticated research skills
— Community liaison
— Fund-raising, grant writing, and fiscal management for budgets of several
  million dollars
— Expertise in political process and political action
— Campaign management for local union and school associations
— Excellent communication skills, both verbal and written
— Member/officer community action organization and local school associations

Employment History

1998–Present	Managing Librarian, Metropolitan Public Library, Chula Vista, CA
1992–1998	Supervising Librarian, Hollywood Branch, Los Angeles County Public Library
1988–1992	Social Sciences Librarian, Westwood Branch, Los Angeles County Public Library
1985–1988	Political Science Fellow, American Federation of State, County and Municipal Employees
1984–1985	Librarian Intern, City of Los Angeles Municipal Library

Education

M.A., University of Southern California, 1985
Political Science/Public Administration
M.S.L.S., University of California, Los Angeles, 1984 (Certified Public Librarian)
B.S., Pepperdine University, 1982
Sociology/Political Science

Other Interests

— International Politics and Government
— Reading
— Travel

REFERENCES MAY BE OBTAINED UPON REQUEST

Career Changer

DOUGLAS ADAMS

32 WEST 24TH STREET • NEW YORK, NEW YORK 10010

(212) 555-6288 (CELL) • DADAMS002@XXX.COM

OBJECTIVE

Real estate sales position with a large agency

QUALIFICATIONS

- Licensed in real estate sales in New York State
- Certificate in real estate from La Guardia Community College
- Twenty-five years experience as home owner and landlord
- Applied knowledge of computer applications and software

RELATED EXPERIENCE

- Trainee in real estate sales, ABCO Realty
- Researched, purchased, and financed own home and developed expertise in same
- Completed comprehensive course in real estate sales at La Guardia Community College
- Marketed and sold retail products and developed good customer relations for over twenty years
- Advised relatives and friends on real estate purchases

EMPLOYMENT HISTORY

1994–Present	Draftsman, Hanson, Jones and Walters, Inc.
1982–1994	Draftsman, Century Drafting and Design
1972–1982	Drafting Technician, Newark Engineering

EDUCATION

- La Guardia Community College, Certificate in Real Estate
- Bramson Technical College, Drafting and Design (12 credits toward A.A.S. degree)
- City College of New York, Blueprint Reading (3 credits)

Career Changer

Myrna J. Myers

1786 Starlight Drive • Newton, MA 05342
Home: 617/555-8932 • Pager: 617/555-3112 • myrnam@xxx.net

Objective

To obtain an entry-level position in public relations.

Education

Bachelor of Science in Business Administration, 1993
Holister State University
Holister, Massachusetts
Major: Public Relations
GPA 3.2

Work Experience

The Meteor Weekly, Langdon, Massachusetts
Advertising Sales Representative, 2000–present
- Responsible for a sales territory consisting of more than 200,000 people.
- Conducted sales canvassing with local merchants, and once sale was made, followed the development of the ad until publication.

The Suntel Communications Co., Langdon, Massachusetts
Receptionist and Advertising Media Assistant, 1993–1999
- Greeted and received clients; scheduled appointments for advertising account representatives on sales leads.

Career Related Activities

Cochairperson for the annual Early American Cultural Festival for the past six years in Holister, Massachusetts. Integrated advertising and local cultural information into a yearly program book, from which all profits are contributed to a local charity.

Advertising Editor for the Holister State University newspaper, 1991–1993.

Seminars & Workshops

Dale Carnegie course in Public Speaking
Newton, Massachusetts, 1999

Creative Writing
Newton, Massachusetts, 1998

Career Changer

YOSHIDO UMEKI

9783 Ridgeway Drive • Evanston, IL 60204 • (847) 555-2983 • umeki@xxx.com

OBJECTIVE

A position as Publicist for a successful popular magazine

SUMMARY OF QUALIFICATIONS

- Excellent public relations skills
- Experienced and published writer
- Accustomed to working on deadline
- Flexible and hardworking
- Knowledgeable about local government, business, and community

HISTORY OF EMPLOYMENT

News Reporter, *Chicago Tribune*, 2000–present

Specialize in local news. Complete assignments and research leads for newsworthy stories. Interview local government officials, corporate officers, community activists, and business owners. Developed the series "On Your Block" for the weekend edition, featuring various local communities. Developed a five-part story exploring community relations of Illinois corporate businesses.

Education Reporter, *Honolulu Star Bulletin*, 1994–2000

Started as a proofreader, within a year had written several feature stories, and within two years obtained responsibility for reporting and researching all education news.

SELECTED LIST OF PUBLICATIONS

- "Hadley and Hadley's Scramble for Community Support"
- "Community Coalition: A Homegrown Response to Woes"
- "Volunteerism: A Way of Life at Wright Brothers"
- "Hawaii's Schools: Rebuilding Promises"
- "Amelia Hunani: A New Breed of Administrator"
- "Tea and Crumpets in the Southeast District"
- "Evanston's Four-Story Community: A Look at North Broadway"
- "WESTAR's Model Community Enrichment Program"

EDUCATION

Bachelor of Arts, Journalism and Government, University of Hawaii at Manoa, Honolulu

REFERENCES AND PUBLICATION PORTFOLIO ON REQUEST

DISLOCATED WORKER

A dislocated worker is a worker who has been laid off from his or her job because the company closed or moved away. These workers are often unable to find new jobs because there is no longer a need for their skills. A good example is workers in the textiles industry. Many textile companies have closed because the United States now imports large amounts of clothing and fabrics. This is due to the fact that labor costs abroad make the price of foreign goods cheaper than the price of those made here. Other industries are affected in the same way.

If you are a dislocated worker, you may have to get training to learn new job skills. You can get this training through a community (two-year) college, a government-funded job training program, or other reputable program. Your library or state employment office has information about where you can get training.

Dislocated workers need to highlight skills that can be used in many different kinds of jobs. All of us have such skills. For example, if you worked in the steel industry, some of your skills might be useful in other manufacturing companies. If you know how to use special equipment or machinery or understand how to use different types of machines, you can probably operate machinery somewhere else. If you have enjoyed teaching others how to operate machinery, you can look for jobs that allow you to train others. If you have experience in other areas, whether or not it was paid experience, include such experience on your resume.

Also, ask yourself some questions.

1. Can I get a job in a different industry because I know about that industry?

2. Are some of the skills I have the same as the skills needed in the new industry?

3. Did I ever do volunteer work? What kinds? Are there any jobs I could get doing the same kind of work?

4. Is there a place I could move to where my industry still operates?

5. Is there something else I could do to make money, like starting my own small business?

6. Do I want to go to school to learn new job skills?

By answering these questions, you can learn more about yourself This will make it easier for you to write a new resume. The following resume examples will also help you.

Dislocated Worker

James W. Lemon

Rural Route 1 • Hastings, Nebraska 68902 • (402) 555-7234 (cell)

AGRICULTURE
—Prepared soil, irrigation water, and plant tissue samples for laboratory analysis.
—Scheduled all purchasing and marketing.
—Implemented nutrition and waste management programs.
—Coordinated all agronomic operations.
—Supervised swine activities.

SUPERVISION AND MANAGEMENT
—Supervised 4 employees.
—Initiated all activities for a swine corporation.
—Managed record-keeping system.

SALES
—Expanded sales by 35% for area livestock nutrition dealers.
—Directed sales, distribution, and created new markets as a livestock nutrition dealer.
—Instructed and motivated dealers and employers.
—Scheduled producer meetings.

LIVESTOCK NUTRITION
—Collected water, complete feed and feedstuff samples for laboratory analysis.
—Analyzed nutritional needs of livestock.

EXTRA ACTIVITIES
—Managed budget and disbursements as church council treasurer for 6 years.
—Led and coordinated County Pork Producers as director and secretary for 3 years.
—Supervised and organized activities as Sunday school teacher for 4 years—grade 3.

EDUCATION AND EXPERIENCE
1997–present	Livestock Nutrition Dealer, Hastings, NE.
1996–present	Self-employed Agriculturalist, Hastings, NE.
1993–1996	Swine Corporation Manager, De-Cla, Inc., Clatonia, NE.
1992–1993	Livestock Nutrition Salesperson, Ralston Purina Co., Omaha, NE.
1991	B.S. in Agriculture—University of Nebraska at Lincoln.

REFERENCES AVAILABLE UPON REQUEST

Dislocated Worker

David Michael Martin, Jr.

Rural Route 2   (515) 555-3276 (cell)
Estherville, IA 51334   dmmartin003@aol.com

Employment Objective

Veterinary Technical or any position where my experience in animal care can be used or expanded.

Experience

2000–Present
On-Call Veterinary Assistant, Adams Veterinary Hospital, Estherville, IA
- Assisted local veterinarian with minor medical emergencies
- Advised area farmers on the proper care and management of their livestock
- Diagnosed livestock and pet diseases
- Instructed local farmers on proper disease prevention and treatment methods
- Delivered newborn calves, hogs, swine, and sheep
- Collected water, complete feed and feedstuff samples for laboratory analysis
- Conducted nutrition and vitamin experiments on area livestock

1988–Present
Self-employed Dairy Farmer, Estherville, IA
- Initiated all administration activities of a dairy farm
- Hired, trained, and supervised 3 employees
- Managed financial record-keeping system
- Analyzed livestock nutritional needs
- Prepared and administered inoculations to control the outbreak and spread of disease
- Managed selection and breeding of dairy cattle through genetic engineering
- Delivered and bottle-nursed newborn calves

Education and Special Training

May 1996	Seminar on Livestock Nutrition. Pioneer Seed Company, Des Moines, IA.
June 1992	Mini-course on Veterinary Medicine. Health-Tech Medical Supplies, Inc., Omaha, NE.
1988	Bachelor of Agriculture, Iowa State University.

Extra Activities

Elected Vice-President, National Dairy Association
Organized Livestock Committee for the Sidney, Iowa, Rodeo
Member, County Agriculture Board
Member, County School Board

Dislocated Worker (Blue-Collar Worker)

Mark C. Barber

1937 Carnegie Drive • Media, PA 19063
(610) 555-9043 (cell) • barbermc@xxx.com

Employment Objective

A position where my skills and expertise in machine maintenance, assembly operations, and shipping/receiving will be significant assets.

Employment History

March 1992 to September 2003, Kaplan Automotive, Nilyania, Ohio
Assembly Operator

- Maintained automotive production equipment on a weekly basis following complex maintenance procedures.
- Used precision measuring equipment on automobile door frames to assure consistent quality production.
- Assembled door frames accurately and consistently.

January 1988 to February 1992, Steadrite Distributors, Grand Isle, Ohio
Shipping Clerk

- Accurately processed paperwork and maintained records of over 100 industrial supply orders per week.
- Devised and refined a complex system of financial and inventory control to ensure effective and profitable warehouse operations.
- Led a Labor-Management working team implementing a "just in time" delivery system.
- Instructed six shipping department assistants in the operation of the delivery system.

Education and Specialized Training

- Chief Clerical Assistant School, Fort Ives, Kentucky, June 1987 to November 1988. Army filing systems, inventory control, and office management.
- Nilyania High School, Nilyania, Ohio. Graduated June 1987.

Honors and Awards

Employee of the Month—Kaplan Automotive, September 2001.
Recognition for team leadership in exceeding door frame production quota for six consecutive months.

1988 Fort Ives Certificate of Initiative awarded by base commander to the enlisted man "whose efforts significantly improved soldier morale."

References available upon request

OLDER WORKER

Age should not be considered a major difficulty for those over forty who are seeking work. In firms with more than twenty employees, workers are protected by the age discrimination law. Older employees with more and broader experience and a greater understanding of the world of work also have an extra edge over younger workers.

In preparing a resume, the older job hunter should emphasize maturity, skills, and experience. Although it is illegal to ask questions about age, a resume without any dates suggests that there may be something to hide and may create the impression that the job seeker is older than he or she really is.

All appropriate dates should be given. But you need not give age or birth date, or year of graduation. Omit publication dates if articles were written several years ago. In short, omit any clues that will screen you out.

Do not list all positions held. Group early work history by type of positions held. Omit unrelated jobs and those held for short periods. Be careful not to leave any time gaps. The resume does not need to be an all-inclusive document. It should not make you look out of date, but it should concentrate on present skills and activities. Only the most recent jobs that will convince an employer of your desirability need be listed. This type of resume should present specific qualifications for the job for which you are applying.

Many counselors suggest a functional resume because it highlights strengths and talents to the best advantage. Whatever format is selected, it should follow the standard directions for good resume writing. It should stress qualifications and experience. It should state the facts truthfully. Above all, it should be positive and present you as an achiever.

Older Worker

John Q. Johnson

738 Highland Avenue
Holyoke, MA 01040
413-555-6468 (office)
413-555-5897 (cell)
johnq@xxx.net

Objective:	Insurance Sales Manager
Management:	Coordinated office operations in six-person agency. Trained clerical staff in processing claims. Developed sales campaign for introduction of new pension plan product. Recruited and trained sales staff.
Sales:	Sold over $5 million in group insurance annually for the last three years. Led agency in monthly volume of sales three times in past year. Analyzed and presented proposals to 100 firms in past 12 months. Contributed to agency that won 2002 Agency of Year award for sales.

Work Experience:

1996–Present	Assistant Manager, Smithers Insurance Agency
1981–1996	Insurance Agent, John Hancock Insurance
Prior to 1981	Held positions in retail sales of appliances and home furnishings

Education:	Northeastern University, B.S. Business Administration Coursework for CLU

Professional Organizations:

National Association of Life Underwriters
Massachusetts Marketing Association

REFERENCES AVAILABLE ON REQUEST

Older Worker

Mary L. Henderson

798 East Haven Road
Hartford, Connecticut 06041
860/555-0921
860/555-4994 (cell)
hendersons@xxx.net

Objective:	Office Manager or Executive Secretary
Work Experience:	
1989–Present	**Office Manager**—Jones and Matthews, Dentists, Inc. Duties include scheduling, bookkeeping, ordering supplies, billing, receptionist duties, and scheduling functions.
1980–1989	**Receptionist**—Dafley, Hoyt, Parsons and Johnson, Attorneys. Duties included switchboard operation, typing, and client contact.
Prior to 1980	**Clerk-Typist**—Simmons Temporary Agency. Held part-time temporary positions during the period when family responsibilities prevented me from holding a full-time position.
Skills:	• Knowledge of all office procedures and equipment. • Word processing: 95 words a minute • Software use: Microsoft Word, WordPerfect, spreadsheets, some HTML • Equipment familiarity: PC, fax machine, dictating equipment, basic office equipment
Education:	• Secretarial Course, Hartford Business College, West Hartford • Adult Education course in word processing and computer applications
Volunteer Activities:	• West Hartford Schools: PTA Secretary, Fund-Raising Committee, Room Mother • Easter Seals: Neighborhood Coordinator • Cub Scouts: Den Mother

REFERENCES AVAILABLE UPON REQUEST

Older Worker

NANCY MANTELLO

6 Horizon Road • Windham, Ohio 44288
216-555-9361 • mantello@xxx.com

RELATED EXPERIENCE

Treasurer, Board of Directors, Horizon House, Windham, Ohio
1997–present
➤ Conserved $80,000 on air-conditioning cooling towers
➤ Arranged a 15-year warranty on building's roof
➤ Brought about the reduction of $2,000,000 escrow mortgage currency
➤ Reviewed and changed the specifications of the contract award for fire doors
➤ Produced substantial savings in the employees' health insurance package
➤ Promoted positive action on the lighting in Riverbank Park, as a consequence of an excellent relationship with the mayor and town council members

WORK HISTORY

Office Manager, Land O' Lakes, Inc., Kent, Ohio
1981–1996
➤ Supervised a clerical staff of 17
➤ Prepared quarterly and annual reports, tax returns, payroll, and warehouse stock replenishment statistics
➤ Directed computerized stock reconciliation and rotation processes
➤ Conducted cash flow, securities analysis, and project feasibility studies
➤ Prepared and directed yearly management seminars
➤ Received several promotions after starting at the company as a clerk

Clerk, Giant Eagle, Inc., Warren, Ohio
1976–1981
➤ Supervised and controlled large amounts of cash flow
➤ Maintained weekly ledgers
➤ Computed figures with speed and accuracy
➤ Maintained activity in customer accounts

EDUCATION

Youngstown State University, Youngstown, Ohio
Courses included Accounting, Business, Typing, and Dictation

WORKER MOVING INTO MANAGEMENT

Climbing the career ladder can be very difficult. Employers want their supervisors and managers to have the experience they need to do the job. If you want to move up the ladder into a management position, you have to write a resume that convinces an employer that you can do the job. It is very important to use action words (see Appendix B) to describe the skills you have. Many times you may also have to use numbers to impress an employer.

Ask yourself the following questions, taking into consideration both your paid and your volunteer work experience:

1. Have I ever supervised other people in a work situation?

2. Was I responsible for handling or managing a budget?

3. Did I ever create a new procedure to use in my job or for my company?

4. Did I ever organize activities, meetings, meals, or conferences for my company or organization?

5. Have I had any courses or other training that relates to the new position I want?

6. Have I been promoted at my company or have each of the jobs that I've had been better than the last?

Were you able to answer yes to these questions? Do you have the facts to back up your answers? If so, then you are probably ready to look for jobs that include supervision and management. Your resume should say that you have the skills you need even if your job titles do not. Make sure you emphasize your knowledge and ability to move into a higher position. You must also say in your cover letter that you are ready to move up and accept the challenges and responsibilities of management.

Worker Moving into Management

Jessica Rooker

8563 Oak Ridge Avenue • Columbus, OH 43215
(614) 555-8305 • (614) 555-6229 (cell) • jbrooker@xxx.com

Objective

A position as Director of a large Human Resources Department

Qualifications

—Screen and interview support personnel in organization employing
1,500 full-time staff.
—Prepare evaluation reports.
—Conduct in-house training programs for support staff (average of
10 yearly).
—Recommend review of department procedures.
—Review and modify organizational staff policies to comply with federal,
state, and local regulations.
—Attend collective bargaining meetings.
—Attend grievance and other personnel-related hearings.
—Assist in recruitment activities on and off site.
—Assist in preparation of department budget.
—Supervise full-time staff of three.

Employment

1996–Present	Drexel Corporation—Department of Human Resources, Department Assistant
1993–1996	Stevens, Inc.—Office of Personnel, Administrative Assistant
1991–1993	Stevens, Inc.—Switchboard Operator

Education

1998–2002	Ohio State University—M.S. Human Resource Administration
1993–1998	Ohio State University—B.S. Counseling and Industrial Relations

Worker Moving into Management

Holly Chen

4133 Center Grove Road

Randolph, NJ 07869

(973) 555-2388 (cell)

hchen77@xxx.com

Objective

Director of Fine and Applied Arts Department

Summary of Qualifications

❯ Over 30 years professional experience in fine and applied arts including fashion, painting, sculpture and ceramics, crafts, decoration, and original design
❯ Successful teacher and program administrator
❯ Lay leader/member of various civic, community, and service organizations
❯ Licensed real estate salesperson

Experience

1973–Present:	Freelance crafts instructor
1996–Present:	Reading tutor for foreign-born children
1973–Present:	Freelance dress tailor and designer of custom-made garments for children and women
1968–1973:	Family management
1993:	Staff advisor: Folk Arts Festival, Girl Scouts of the USA
1985–1988:	District Commissioner, Girl Scout Council of New Jersey
1983–1985:	Assistant District Commissioner, Girl Scout Council of New Jersey
1977–1985:	Troop leader, Girl Scout Council of greater New York
1966–1968:	Draper and assistant designer, Adrian's of Hollywood, Hollywood, California

Education

2001:	Small business management course (certificate), New School for Social Research
1995:	Real estate sales licensing course (license)
1966–1968:	Fashion Institute of Technology (15 credits completed toward A.A.S. degree)
1962–1966:	Textile Trades High School, Los Angeles, CA (diploma)

REFERENCES FURNISHED UPON REQUEST

Worker Moving into Management

Claire Simmonds
423 Wilson Avenue
Pittsburgh, PA 15218
(412) 555-7772 (cell)
clairesimm@xxx.com

OBJECTIVE
Position as Administrative Assistant

EXPERIENCE
January 1996–August 2003
Lay Administrator, St. Benedict the Moor Church, Pittsburgh, PA
Entered computerized school records; updated approximately 150 financial records weekly; organized and managed recreational program for 350 students weekly; ordered supplies; scheduled volunteers; handled money. Also responsible for monthly accounting, filing, and budgeting.

October 1982–January 1996
Assistant Sales Service Director, KDYV-TV, Pittsburgh, PA
Duties included: preparing a daily computerized commercial log, booking orders, filing, working with salespeople mainly via telephone to set up replacement spots.

Prior to 1982
Deposit Accounting Clerk, Union Bank, Pittsburgh, PA
Filed checks, verified signatures, rendered monthly statements.

VOLUNTEER EXPERIENCE
Chair, St. Benedict the Moor School Board
Board Member, Heights District Federal Credit Union
Board Member, Diocesan School Board

EDUCATION
St. John the Baptist High School
Diploma

REFERENCES
Available upon request

RESUMES FOR SPANISH SPEAKERS

Muchas veces las personas olvidan que tienen aptitudes las cuales pueden ayudarlos a conseguir empleos de mejor pago aunque no hayan sido entrenados para un oficio especifico. Comúnmente, estas aptitudes pueden ser relacionadas a un empleo.

Algunas de estas habilidades son:

1. Conocimiento de idiomas además del inglés.

2. Una licencia de manejar válida.

3. Poder llevarse bien con otras personas.

4. Tener la experiencia de haber trabajado en grupo con niños y adultos.

5. Poder supervisar otras personas (niños o adultos).

6. Pasatiempos o aficiones.

7. Haber viajado.

8. Haber leído libros o revistas sobre los tipos de trabajos o oficios en los que usted quiere trabajar.

Los resúmenes siguientes fueron escritos para personas que tienen algún tipo de experiencia laboral, pero poco entrenamiento. Vea como incluyen aptitudes y requisitos que no se desempeñaron en el trabajo mismo.

Si usted no tiene las habilidades necesarias para trabajar en un empleo técnico, de oficio o profesional, todavía puede escribir un resumen que cause una buena impresión a un patrón debido a que usted está conciente de sus aptitudes y talentos, lo cual también es importante.

GUIA PARA UN RESUMEN SIMPLE EN ORDEN CRONOLÓGICO

Aquí son ejemplos de los secciónes incluir en su resumen. Empieza con su nombre, dirección y teléfono.

NOMBRE
Dirección
Ciudad, Estado
Código postal
Teléfono

Diga en breve el tipo de posición que busca, como ésta se relacione con su educación, su experiencia y sus intereses. Pueda usar "Objetivo de Carrera," u "Objetivo de Empleo" tambien.

Busco posición que utilice mis habilidades.

Busco posición que utilice mis antecedentes y experiencia y que utilice mis extensos conocimientos de _____.

Incluya un sección que da su experiencia de trabajo. En esta sección diga el titulo, nombre de compañía, localidad y fechas de cada empleo que tuvo (comience con el empleo más reciente). Use frases brevas y activas para describir las tareas y obligaciones. Prepare una lista de sus logros y contribuciones. Ud. puede incluir sus contribuciones voluntarias. Use descripciones separadas para cada posición desempeñada dentro de la misma compañía, incluyendo fechas y promociones.

Experiencia Laboral

1999 - presente
Recepcionista--Texaco, Inc. Dallas, Texas
Obligaciones: Contesto a teléfono, respondo los questiones de los clientes, uso la compulatora cada día.

"Otra Experiencia" es una sección opcional, en que se incluyen empleos anteriores o trabajo no relacionado. Use descripciones muy breves. Más vale no incluir esta experiencia si el titulo de la clasificación es evidente por si mismo.

"Educación" es otra titulo académico, especialización de curso, si está relacionada con el empleo, institución académica (escuela secundaria, colegio o universidad), acto de graduación, promedio, de calificación si superior a 3.0. Incluya su educación si ha tomado cursos de adulto, su adiestramiento de trabajo, seminarios y conferencias, clases vocacionales, y cursos especializados si se relacionan con el empleo.

Educación

Secundaria Diploma
Central High School, Chicago, Illinois
Graduación: 1999

Hechos personales es otra sección opcional, para información tal, como el hecho de que podría establecerse en un nuevo lugar, el deseo de hacer viajes, participación en las actividades de la comunidad, dominio de una lengua extranjera (también se puede incluir en la sección de Educación), intereses que se relacionan con el empleo, habilidades, las actividades en que le gusta participar durante su tiempo libre.

El Trabajador con Habilidades Poco Elevadas

Martin Melendez

345 West Fourth Street
Dayton, Ohio 45402
(937) 555-8664 (cell)

Objetivo

Obtener una posición como empleado de surtido en una amplia organización de venta al por menor.

Habilidades

- Administrar el movimiento de grandes volúmenes de mercancía.
- Supervisar el inventario y preparar reportes inventaríales.
- Operar maquinarias de almacenes y equipo empaquetador.
- Preciso con cifras.
- Formal y confiable.
- Habilidad para aprender rápidamente.
- Capaz de asumir nuevas responsabilidades.
- Bien organizado y eficiente.
- Bilingüe en español e inglés.

Historial de Empleo

2000–Al Presente: Empleado de Mercancía, ACME Supermarkets, Almacén Principal, Livingston, Ohio

1998–2000: Empleado de Surtidos, Laurel Drug Store. Dayton, Ohio Repartidor, Laurel Drug Store.

Educación

2002: Diploma de equivalencia secundaria, Cincinnati Central Vocational High School.
Cursos en mantenimiento de edificios y reparación.

El Trabajador de Edad

MARY L. HENDERSON

698 ADAMS ROAD • WEST HARTFORD, CT 06041
860-555-9921 • 860-555-8833 (CELL)
MLHENDERSON@XXX.NET

OBJETIVO

Administradora de Oficina o Secretaria Ejecutiva.

EXPERIENCIA LABORAL

1999–Al Presente   Administradora de Oficina—Jones and Matthews, Dentist, Inc. Obligaciones: llevar los horarios, teneduría de libros órdenes de provisiones, cobro de cuentas, recepcionista y programadora de funciones.

1994–1999   Recepcionista—Daily, Hoyt, Parsons and Johnson, Attorneys. Obligaciones: operadora de cuadro de mandos, mecanografía y contacto con clientes.

Antes de 1994   Recepcionista—Mecanografía—Simmons Temporary Agency. Trabajo a medio tiempo con posiciones temporarias durante un período en el que obligaciones familiares no me permitieron mantener una posición de tiempo completo.

HABILIDADES

Conocimiento, de procedimientos oficinales y equipos mecanografía: 90 palabras por minuto. Procesamiento de palabras y uso de programas y sistemas de programación PC como Word, Excel, Access.

EDUCACIÓN

A. S., Hartford Business College, West Hartford.
Un curso de educación adulta en procesamiento de palabras y aplicaciones de computadoras.

SERVICIOS VOLUNTARIOS

West Hartford Schools: Secretaria PTA, Comité de levantamiento de fondos, ayudante en la clase de mis hijos. Easter Cub Scouts: Madrina de cubil.

Las referencias están disponibles bajo petición.

OUTSTANDING SAMPLE RESUME FRAGMENTS

The following samples are taken from resumes covering a variety of positions. For the sake of simplicity, these examples omit the full resume information, but instead focus on representative ways to describe qualifications, previous job duties, and other important information. Use these samples as examples for developing key portions of your own resume.

JOB AREA: SECURITY

Focus: Skill areas

- *Highly experienced in various aspects of protecting property and personnel*

- *Skilled in performing physical security inspections*

- *Closely familiar with effective procedures for reducing threats, anticipating security problems, and dealing with contemporary security issues*

- *Skilled in using fire equipment, weapons, locks, alarms, and other devices and equipment related to security*

- *Adept at various self-defense measures*

- *Highly reliable in following orders, implementing procedures, and acting independently when needed*

JOB AREA: SURVEYING

Focus: Previous job tasks

In role as topographic surveyor for large geological services company, completed tasks such as the following:

—Recorded topographic survey data

—Operated variety of survey instruments

—Performed topographic and geodetic computations

—Interpreted maps and aerial photographs

—Performed a wide range of computations including horizontal differences, angular closures, and triangulations

—Prepared technical and personnel reports

JOB AREA: GRAPHIC DESIGN

Focus: Related skills

■ Highly experienced in graphic design and illustration

■ Experienced in various techniques (both hand and computer-aided) for developing illustrations for posters, graphs, charts, training aids, brochures, books, and other publications as well as for electronic media

■ Accomplished in using a variety of traditional media including pencil, pen and ink, water color, art markers, and other media

■ Skilled in use of the latest software and computer equipment for graphics, desktop publishing, Web design, and related areas

■ Adept at producing both realistic and cartoon-style drawings and other illustrations

■ Highly flexible in completing different types of assignments, working with others, and using creativity in practical applications

JOB AREA: EQUIPMENT REPAIR

Focus: Job duties performed

- Perfomed general maintenance and repairs on computers, printers, scanners, and other electronic equipment
- Inspected and tested equipment and componenents
- Diagnosed and repaired malfunctions both in shop and in the field
- Performed troubleshooting and adjustment of electromechanical devices in digital systems
- Prepared maintenance schedules for electronic data equipment
- Effectively utilized various hand tools and electronic equipment

JOB AREA: MACHINE TOOL TECHNOLOGY

Focus: Job duties performed

- Set up and operated machine tools
- Made and repaired metal parts, mechanisms, and machinery using both traditional and computer-controlled techniques
- Supervised two other workers in setting up and using equipment
- Assisted supervisor in managing shop operations
- Performed comprehensive duties requiring firsthand knowledge of metalworking techniques

JOB AREA: PUBLIC RELATIONS

Focus: Brief qualifications summary followed by detailed listing of accomplishments

CAPABILITIES

Energetic, articulate public relations professional. Skilled in all aspects of writing, designing, editing, and producing publications. Experienced in writing news releases, print ads, newsletters, and other material. Adept at developing Web-based material.

ACHIEVEMENTS

- Developed award-winning series of publications offered by Virginia Community College System (VCCS)

- Completed writing, design, and layout for more than 150 publications for two public community colleges

- Initiated expanded community relations program designed to foster good relations with area businesses and nonprofit organizations

- Designed and wrote E-newsletter for community college alumni

- Received "Outstanding Communicator Award" from Virginia Association of Educational Public Relations Practitioners

JOB AREA: MEDICAL LABORATORY TECHNOLOGY

Focus: Job skills

Thoroughly experienced in:

– *procurement of blood samples*
– *various types of testing including leukocyte differential, hemoglobin and hematocrit testing analysis*
– *effective blood storage and shipment techniques*
– *other standard practices*

JOB AREA: ANY

Focus: Volunteerism

Volunteer, Special Olympics, Ames, Iowa

Active in "Big Sister" program, Des Moines, Iowa

Volunteer on church mission trips to coastal South Carolina (repairing poverty housing)

JOB AREA: FINANCIAL MANAGEMENT

Focus: Tasks performed

- *Conducted field audits of state agencies and regional offices*
- *Examined financial and program records*
- *Wrote audit reports*
- *Communicated audit findings to agencies and state officials*
- *Played key role in designing computerized auditing management system*

JOB AREA: EDITING

Focus: Job history and key tasks performed

EMPLOYMENT HISTORY

1998–2003 Copyeditor, *The Washington Post*, Washington, D.C.

Duties: Performed general copyediting duties required for publication of classified ads on a daily basis. Reviewed and revised materials prior to publication. Consulted with other editors and outside contacts in clarifying technical details or verbal ambiguities.

1994–1998 Editorial Assistant, National Endowment for the Humanities, Washington, D.C.

Duties: Performed general editorial duties. Assisted in editing reports, newsletters, requests for proposals, and other publications.

1993-94 Part-Time Copyeditor, *Association Weekly*, Alexandria, VA.

Duties: Assisted editor in general copyediting.

JOB AREA: PURCHASING

Focus: Job skills

◆ Skilled in all aspects of purchasing including quality control, bidding, acquisition of equipment, and records management

◆ Experienced in using personal computers and various office equipment

◆ Skilled in vendor selection, inventory, and supplier relations

◆ Experienced in dealing with international purchasing practices

JOB AREA: SECRETARIAL

Focus: Job skills

> ❖ *Highly experienced in operating various types of office equipment*
>
> ❖ *Proficient in typing/word processing, averaging more than 80 words per minute*
>
> ❖ *Adept at using several word processing and office management software programs*
>
> ❖ *Highly efficient in maintaining correspondence records and filing systems*
>
> ❖ *Skilled in telephone management, customer/client relations, and maintaining efficient oral and written communications, both internal and external*

JOB AREA: RECREATION

Focus: Job skills/experience

> • Highly experienced in various aspects of planning and carrying out recreation programs
>
> • Experienced in both traditional athletics and outdoor innovative "adventure" programming
>
> • Flexible in reaching children, youths, and adult audiences
>
> • Effective in supervising subordinates, including part-time and volunteer workers
>
> • Highly knowledgeable of effective marketing techniques
>
> • Experienced in budgeting and fund management
>
> • Experienced in developing community partnerships and making maximum use of resources in support of recreation programming

JOB AREA: CONSTRUCTION

Focus: Details of previous experience

◆ Fabricated, erected, and maintained/repaired wooden and masonry structures for federal housing project

◆ Performed complex construction activities including interpreting blueprints, estimating material needs, and installing finished carpentry product

◆ Mastered used of a variety of tools including power tools

◆ Performed a comprehensive array of tasks including erection of building components such as floors, roofing systems, walls, and stairs

◆ Completed both rough and finish work while working in a timely fashion

JOB AREA: PHARMACY ASSISTANT

Focus: Details of previous experience

— Highly experienced in providing support to pharmacists by assisting in preparing, controlling, and issuing pharmaceutical products.
— Assisted pharmacists in performing a wide range of duties.
— Compounded and filled prescription orders.
— Performed storage, accounting, inventory, and control procedures.
— Issued medications under pharmacists' supervision.
— Maintained stock levels and ordered supplies.
— Performed other related duties.

JOB AREA: ELECTRICAL/UTILITY FIELD WORK

Focus: Previous duties performed

- Performed a variety of duties involved in installing, maintaining, and repairing electrical cables and communication lines
- Erected utility poles
- Operated mechanical lifts, plows, and other equipment
- Installed overhead communications and electrical cables between utility poles
- Installed street lights and other lighting systems
- Spliced and sealed cables for watertightness
- Installed voltage regulators, electrical transformers, and voltage regulators
- Performed related duties

JOB AREA: SHEET METAL CONSTRUCTION

Focus: Brief summary of qualifications

Highly experienced sheet metal worker with six years of experience at Fairchild Industries. Adept at using proper techniques for top quality sheet metal work. Very dependable and productive.

JOB AREA: PLUMBING

Focus: Succinct list of tasks performed

—*Performed basic plumbing services*
—*Installed and maintained simple and complex pipe systems*
—*Installed various plumbing fixtures*
—*Performed other plumbing-related tasks*

JOB AREA: COUNSELING

Focus: Brief qualifications summary

- Highly adept at working with people
- Experienced in counseling persons with various problems/needs
- Skilled in interviewing techniques, administration and scoring of psychological tests, and other counseling strategies
- Experienced in screening and evaluating persons with substance abuse problems, and assisting in managing substance abuse programs

JOB AREA: MANAGEMENT

Focus: Educational credentials

M.B.A., University of Virginia, Charlottesville, Virginia, 2002.

B.S., Emory and Henry College, Emory, Virginia, 2000.
Graduated in top 10 percent of class.
Major: Business Management.

A.A., Wytheville Community College, Wytheville, VA, 1998. Earned 3.9 grade point average (4.0 scale) in general studies (transfer) curriculum.

Completed additional studies at North Carolina State University (six graduate credits in marketing research).

JOB AREA: PHOTOGRAPHY

Focus: Specific job skills

Skilled in:

—*photographic lab techniques*

—*lab supervision*

—*digital photography*

—*color photography*

—*illustrative photography*

—*aerial photography*

—*photojournalism*

—*portraiture*

—*other photographic skills/techniques*

JOB AREA: RADIOGRAPHY

Focus: Brief qualifications summary

Experienced medical radiographer. Fully licensed and registered. Skilled in operating state-of-the-art radiographic equipment for diagnosis and treatment of medical conditions. Experienced in practicing effective patient relations and interacting with other health care staff.

JOB AREA: DENTAL HYGIENE

Focus: Brief summary of accomplishments

> *Served successfully for large dental practice in metropolitan Chicago as a dental hygienist. Received outstanding performance evaluations. Served in volunteer capacity through special program providing dental care for disadvantaged children.*

JOB AREA: MARKETING

Focus: Educational credentials

B.S., University of Kentucky, Lexington, Kentucky, 1996
Major: Business Marketing
Minor: Mathematics
G.P.A.: 3.6

M.S. in Marketing, University of South Carolina, Columbia, South Carolina, 2001

Additional training obtained through various short-term courses and seminars (complete list available)

Appendix A
For Further Reading

Abel, Alicia. *Business Grammar, Style and Usage: The Desk Reference for Articulate and Polished Business Writing, Speaking and Correspondence.* Aspatore Books, 2003.

Adams, Bob. *The Everything Job Interview Book.* Adams Media Corporation, 2001.

Adams, Bob, and Laura Morin. *The Complete Resume and Job Search Book for College Students.* Adams Media Corporation, 1999.

Allen, Jeffrey G. *The Resume Makeover.* John Wiley and Sons, 2001.

Beatty, Richard H. *175 High-Impact Cover Letters.* John Wiley and Sons, 2002.

Beatty, Richard H. *How to Write a Resume If You Didn't Go to College.* John Wiley and Sons, 2003.

Beatty, Richard H. *The Perfect Cover Letter.* John Wiley and Sons, 1996.

Bernard Haldane Associates. *Haldane's Best Cover Letters for Professionals.* Impact Publications, 1999.

Besson, Tannee S., and National Business Employment Weekly. *Cover Letters.* John Wiley and Sons, 1999.

Besson, Tannee S., and National Business Employment Weekly. *Resumes.* John Wiley and Sons, 1999.

Bloch, Deborah Perlmutter. *How to Get Your First Job and Keep It.* VGM Career Books, 2002.

Block, Jay. *101 Best Cover Letters.* McGraw-Hill, 1999.

Block, Jay. *101 Best Resumes to Sell Yourself.* McGraw-Hill, 2002.

Bolles, Richard Nelson. *What Color Is Your Parachute 2003: A Practical Manual for Job-Hunters and Career-Changers.* Ten Speed Press, 2002.

Brown, Lola. *Resume Writing Made Easy.* Pearson Education, 2002.

Criscito, Pat. *Designing the Perfect Resume.* Barron's Educational Series, 2000.

Cunningham, John R. *The Inside Scoop: Recruiters Share Their Tips on Job Search Success with College Students.* McGraw-Hill, 2001.

Deluca, Matthew J. *Best Answers to the 201 Most Frequently Asked Interview Questions.* McGraw-Hill, 1996.

Devine, Felice Primeau. *Goof Proof Resume and Cover Letter.* Delmar Publishers, 2003.

Drake, John D. *The Perfect Interview: How to Get the Job You Really Want.* Fine Publications, 2002.

Enelow, Wendy S. *Best Keywords for Resumes, Cover Letters, and Interviews: Powerful Communications Tools for Success.* Impact Publications, 2003.

Enelow, Wendy S., and Louise Kursmark. *Cover Letter Magic.* JIST Works, 2000.

Eisenberg, Ronni. *Organize Your Job Search!* Hyperion Press, 2000.

Farr, J. Michael. *The Quick Resume and Cover Letter Book.* JIST Works, Inc., 2000.

Garber, Janet. *Getting a Job.* Silver Lining Books, 2003.

Graber, Steven, and Barry Littmann. *Everything Online Job Search Book: Find the Jobs, Send Your Resume and Land the Career of Your Dreams —All Online!* Adams Media Corporation, 2000.

Greene, Susan D., and Melanie C. Martel. *The Ultimate Job Hunter's Guidebook.* Houghton Mifflin Company, 2000.

Hawley, Casey Fitts. *Effective Letters for Every Occasion.* Barron's Educational Series, 2000.

Holcombe, Marya. *The Best Letter Book Ever.* Round Lake Publishing, 2002.

Iacone, Salvatore J. *Write to the Point: How to Communicate with Style and Purpose.* Career Press, 2003.

Ireland, Susan. *The Complete Idiot's Guide to the Perfect Resume.* The Penguin Group, 2000.

Isaacs, Kim, and Karen Hofferber. *The Career Change Resume.* McGraw-Hill, 2003.

Kennedy, Joyce Lain. *Cover Letters for Dummies.* John Wiley and Sons, 2000.

Krannich, Ronald L., and Caryl Rae Krannich. *Dynamite Cover Letters.* Impact Publications, 1999.

Krannich, Ronald L., and Caryl Rae Krannich. *The Savvy Resume Writer: The Behavioral Advantage.* Impact Publications, 1999.

Lamb, Sandra. *How to Write It: A Complete Guide to Everything You'll Ever Write.* Ten Speed Press, 1998.

Marcus, John, J. *The Resume Makeover: 50 Common Problems with Resumes and Cover Letters—and How to Fix Them.* McGraw-Hill, 2003.

McKinney, Anne, Editored. *Cover Letters That Blow Doors Open.* PREP Publishing, 1999.

McKinney, Anne, Editored. *Real Resumes for Career Changers: Actual Resumes and Cover Letters.* PREP Publishing, 2000.

McKinney, Anne, Editored. *Resumes and Cover Letters for Managers: Job-Winning Resumes and Letters for Management Positions.* PREP Publishing, 1999.

Merhish, Ferris E. 7,001 *Resumes: The Job Search Workbook.* 1st Books Library, 2001.

Nadler, Burton Jay. *The Everything Resume Book.* Adams Media Corporation, 2003.

Nichols, Harve L., and Wallter L. Fortson. *Resume Writing Without Paid Work Experience.* Trafford Publishing, 2001.

Noble, David F. *Gallery of Best Cover Letters: A Collection of Quality Cover Letters by Professional Resume Writers.* JIST Works, 2000.

O'Neill, Lucy. *Job Smarts.* Scholastic Library Publishing, 2001.

Otfinoski, Steve. *Scholastic Guide to Putting It in Writing.* Scholastic, 1993.

Provenzano, Steve. *Blue Collar Resumes.* Career Press, 1999.

Resumes for First-Time Job Hunters. VGM Career Books, 2000.

Resumes for Re-Entering the Job Market. VGM Career Books, 2002.

Rosenberg, Arthur, and David Hizer. *The Resume Handbook: How to Write Outstanding Resumes and Cover Letters for Every Situation.* Adams Media Corporation, 1996.

Swager, Peggy O. *Surviving the 15-Second Resume Read.* Hi-Caliber Books, 2003.

Troutman, Kathryn Kraemer. *Electronic Federal Resume Guidebook.* The Resume Place, 2001.

Troutman, Kathryn Kraemer, and others. *Ten Steps to a Federal Job: Navigating the Federal Job System, Writing Federal Resumes, Ksas and Cover Letters with a Mission.* The Resume Place, 2002.

Washington, Tom. *Resume Power: Selling Yourself on Paper in the New Millennium.* Mount Vernon Press, 2003.

Weber, Karl, and Rob Kaplan. *The Insider's Guide to Writing the Perfect Resume.* Peterson's, 2001.

Webster's New World Letter Writing Handbook. John Wiley and Sons, 2003.

Whitcomb, Susan Britton. *Resume Magic.* JIST Works, 2002.

Whitcomb, Susan Britton, and Pat Kendall. *E-Resumes: Everything You Need to Know About Using Electronic Resumes to Tap into Today's Hot Job Market.* McGraw-Hill, 2001.

Wynett, Stanley. *Cover Letters That Will Get You the Job You Want.* F & W Publications, 1993.

Yate, Martin John. *Resumes That Knock 'em Dead!* Adams Media Corporation, 2000.

Appendix B
Action Words

When writing your resume, you should try to use as many action words (verbs) as you can. Action words liven up your resume and make it more interesting and readable to employers. Following are some action words (each given in three different forms) that you may wish to use in your resume.

accelerate
    accelerated
    accelerating
accomplish
    accomplished
    accomplishing
account
    accounted
    accounting
achieve
    achieved
    achieving
act
    acted
    acting
adapt
    adapted
    adapting
adjust
    adjusted
    adjusting

administer
    administered
    administering
advertise
    advertised
    advertising
advise
    advised
    advising
advocate
    advocated
    advocating
alter
    altered
    altering
analyze
    analyzed
    analyzing
appraise
    appraised
    appraising

approve
  approved
  approving
arbitrate
  arbitrated
  arbitrating
arrange
  arranged
  arranging
assemble
  assembled
  assembling
assign
  assigned
  assigning
assist
  assisted
  assisting
audit
  audited
  auditing
beautify
  beautified
  beautifying
budget
  budgeted
  budgeting
build
  built
  building
buy
  bought
  buying
calculate
  calculated
  calculating
carve
  carved
  carving
catalog
  cataloged
  cataloging
chart
  charted
  charting

check
  checked
  checking
classify
  classified
  classifying
clean
  cleaned
  cleaning
coach
  coached
  coaching
collate
  collated
  collating
collect
  collected
  collecting
command
  commanded
  commanding
communicate
  communicated
  communicating
compare
  compared
  comparing
complete
  completed
  completing
compose
  composed
  composing
compound
  compounded
  compounding
compute
  computed
  computing
conceptualize
  conceptualized
  conceptualizing
conduct
  conducted
  conducting

confront
   confronted
   confronting
conserve
   conserved
   conserving
construct
   constructed
   constructing
consult
   consulted
   consulting
contact
   contacted
   contacting
contribute
   contributed
   contributing
control
   controlled
   controlling
convert
   converted
   converting
cook
   cooked
   cooking
cooperate
   cooperated
   cooperating
coordinate
   coordinated
   coordinating
copy
   copied
   copying
correspond
   corresponded
   corresponding
counsel
   counseled
   counseling
count
   counted
   counting

create
   created
   creating
critique
   critiqued
   critiquing
defend
   defended
   defending
delegate
   delegated
   delegating
deliver
   delivered
   delivering
demonstrate
   demonstrated
   demonstrating
design
   designed
   designing
detect
   detected
   detecting
determine
   determined
   determining
develop
   developed
   developing
devise
   devised
   devising
diagnose
   diagnosed
   diagnosing
direct
   directed
   directing
discover
   discovered
   discovering
dispense
   dispensed
   dispensing

display
   displayed
   displaying
distribute
   distributed
   distributing
divert
   diverted
   diverting
double
   doubled
   doubling
draft
   drafted
   drafting
dramatize
   dramatized
   dramatizing
draw
   drew
   drawing
drive
   drove
   driving
edit
   edited
   editing
eliminate
   eliminated
   eliminating
encourage
   encouraged
   encouraging
enforce
   enforced
   enforcing
enter
   entered
   entering
entertain
   entertained
   entertaining
establish
   established
   establishing

estimate
   estimated
   estimating
evaluate
   evaluated
   evaluating
examine
   examined
   examining
exchange
   exchanged
   exchanging
execute
   executed
   executing
exercise
   exercised
   exercising
exhibit
   exhibited
   exhibiting
expand
   expanded
   expanding
experiment
   experimented
   experimenting
explain
   explained
   explaining
express
   expressed
   expressing
facilitate
   facilitated
   facilitating
feed
   fed
   feeding
file
   filed
   filing
find
   found
   finding

fix
    fixed
    fixing
follow
    followed
    following
forecast
    forecast
    forecasting
formulate
    formulated
    formulating
gain
    gained
    gaining
gather
    gathered
    gathering
generate
    generated
    generating
give
    gave
    giving
guard
    guarded
    guarding
guide
    guided
    guiding
handle
    handled
    handling
harvest
    harvested
    harvesting
heal
    healed
    healing
help
    helped
    helping
identify
    identified
    identifying

imagine
    imagined
    imagining
implement
    implemented
    implementing
improve
    improved
    improving
increase
    increased
    increasing
influence
    influenced
    influencing
initiate
    initiated
    initiating
innovate
    innovated
    innovating
inspect
    inspected
    inspecting
inspire
    inspired
    inspiring
install
    installed
    installing
instruct
    instructed
    instructing
interpret
    interpreted
    interpreting
interview
    interviewed
    interviewing
introduce
    introduced
    introducing
invent
    invented
    inventing

investigate
  investigated
  investigating
judge
  judged
  judging
landscape
  landscaped
  landscaping
launch
  launched
  launching
lay
  laid
  laying
lead
  led
  leading
learn
  learned
  learning
lift
  lifted
  lifting
listen
  listened
  listening
loan
  loaned
  loaning
locate
  located
  locating
mail
  mailed
  mailing
maintain
  maintained
  maintaining
manage
  managed
  managing
measure
  measured
  measuring

mediate
  mediated
  mediating
meet
  met
  meeting
memorize
  memorized
  memorizing
mentor
  mentored
  mentoring
merchandise
  merchandised
  merchandising
message
  messaged
  messaging
model
  modeled
  modeling
modify
  modified
  modifying
monitor
  monitored
  monitoring
motivate
  motivated
  motivating
move
  moved
  moving
negotiate
  negotiated
  negotiating
obtain
  obtained
  obtaining
operate
  operated
  operating
order
  ordered
  ordering

organize
  organized
  organizing
pack
  packed
  packing
package
  packaged
  packaging
paint
  painted
  painting
patrol
  patrolled
  patrolling
perform
  performed
  performing
persuade
  persuaded
  persuading
plan
  planned
  planning
plant
  planted
  planting
plaster
  plastered
  plastering
play
  played
  playing
polish
  polished
  polishing
pose
  posed
  posing
post
  posted
  posting
preach
  preached
  preaching

prepare
  prepared
  preparing
prescribe
  prescribed
  prescribing
present
  presented
  presenting
preside
  presided
  presiding
prevent
  prevented
  preventing
print
  printed
  printing
process
  processed
  processing
produce
  produced
  producing
program
  programmed
  programming
project
  projected
  projecting
promote
  promoted
  promoting
propose
  proposed
  proposing
protect
  protected
  protecting
provide
  provided
  providing
pump
  pumped
  pumping

purchase
    purchased
    purchasing
question
    questioned
    questioning
quote
    quoted
    quoting
raise
    raised
    raising
read
    read
    reading
realize
    realized
    realizing
receive
    received
    receiving
recognize
    recognized
    recognizing
recommend
    recommended
    recommending
record
    recorded
    recording
recruit
    recruited
    recruiting
redesign
    redesigned
    redesigning
reduce
    reduced
    reducing
refer
    referred
    referring
register
    registered
    registering

rehabilitate
    rehabilitated
    rehabilitating
relieve
    relieved
    relieving
remember
    remembered
    remembering
remove
    removed
    removing
render
    rendered
    rendering
reorganize
    reorganized
    reorganizing
repair
    repaired
    repairing
repeat
    repeated
    repeating
replace
    replaced
    replacing
report
    reported
    reporting
represent
    represented
    representing
research
    researched
    researching
restore
    restored
    restoring
review
    reviewed
    reviewing
revise
    revised
    revising

revitalize
>revitalized
>revitalizing

ride
>rode
>riding

route
>routed
>routing

run
>ran
>running

save
>saved
>saving

schedule
>scheduled
>scheduling

sculpt
>sculpted
>sculpting

seat
>seated
>seating

select
>selected
>selecting

sell
>sold
>selling

send
>sent
>sending

serve
>served
>serving

service
>serviced
>servicing

sew
>sewed
>sewing

shampoo
>shampooed
>shampooing

shape
>shaped
>shaping

shave
>shaved
>shaving

simplify
>simplified
>simplifying

sing
>sang
>singing

sketch
>sketched
>sketching

solve
>solved
>solving

sort
>sorted
>sorting

speak
>spoke
>speaking

start
>started
>starting

streamline
>streamlined
>streamlining

strengthen
>strengthened
>strengthening

stress
>stressed
>stressing

stretch
>stretched
>stretching

structure
>structured
>structuring

study
>studied
>studying

style
  styled
  styling
succeed
  succeeded
  succeeding
suggest
  suggested
  suggesting
summarize
  summarized
  summarizing
supersede
  superseded
  superseding
supervise
  supervised
  supervising
supply
  supplied
  supplying
support
  supported
  supporting
survey
  surveyed
  surveying
swim
  swam
  swimming
synthesize
  synthesized
  synthesizing
tailor
  tailored
  tailoring
talk
  talked
  talking
teach
  taught
  teaching
tend
  tended
  tending

terminate
  terminated
  terminating
test
  tested
  testing
time
  timed
  timing
tint
  tinted
  tinting
tolerate
  tolerated
  tolerating
trace
  traced
  tracing
track
  tracked
  tracking
trade
  traded
  trading
train
  trained
  training
transcribe
  transcribed
  transcribing
transfer
  transferred
  transferring
treat
  treated
  treating
trim
  trimmed
  trimming
triple
  tripled
  tripling
tune
  tuned
  tuning

turn
   turned
   turning
tutor
   tutored
   tutoring
type
   typed
   typing
usher
   ushered
   ushering
verify
   verified
   verifying
visualize
   visualized
   visualizing

wash
   washed
   washing
weigh
   weighed
   weighing
welcome
   welcomed
   welcoming
widen
   widened
   widening
win
   won
   winning
wrap
   wrapped
   wrapping